MISSION IN A BROKEN WRLD

REPORT OF ACC-8:
WALES 1990

Published for the Anglican Consultative Council

Published 1990 for the Anglican Consultative Council, Partnership House, 157 Waterloo Road, London SE1 8UT.

This edition by Church House Publishing
Church House, Great Smith Street, London SW1P 3NZ

ISBN 0 7151 4797 8

Printed by Tasprint Limited, South Woodford, London E18 1HB.

THE INTER-ANGLICAN PUBLISHING NETWORK

AUSTRALIA	Anglican Information Office, St Andrew's House, Sydney Square, Sydney 2000
CANADA	Anglican Book Centre, 600 Jarvis Street, Toronto, Ontario M4Y 2J6
GHANA	Anglican Press Ltd, PO Box 8, Accra
INDIA	ISPCK, PO Box 1585, Kashmere Gate, Delhi 11006
KENYA	Uzima Press Ltd, PO Box 48127, Nairobi
NEW ZEALAND	Church of the Province of New Zealand, Box 37-050, Auckland
NIGERIA	CSS Press, 50 Broad Street, PO Box 174, Lagos
SOUTHERN AND CENTRAL AFRICA	Publications Committee, CPSA, PO Box 4849, Johannesburg 2000
TANZANIA	Central Tanganyika Press, PO Box 1129, Dodoma
UGANDA	Centenary Publishing House, PO Box 2776, Kampala
UK	Church House Publishing, Church House, Great Smith Street, London SW1P 3NZ
USA	Forward Movement Publications, 412 Sycamore Street, Cincinnati, Ohio 45202

Contents

Abbreviations used in this Report

ACC	Anglican Consultative Council
ALC	International Anglican Liturgical Consultation
ALICC	Anglican–Lutheran International Continuation Committee
A/OJDD	Anglican/Orthodox Joint Doctrinal Discussions
ARCIC	Anglican Roman Catholic International Commission
BCMS	Bible Churchmen's Missionary Society
BCP	Book of Common Prayer
BEM	*Baptism, eucharist and ministry* (World Council of Churches)
CMS	Church Missionary Society
CPSA	Church of the Province of Southern Africa
ECUSA	Episcopal Church in the United States of America
IAIN	Inter-Anglican Information Network
IATDC	Inter-Anglican Theological and Doctrinal Commission
ICAOTD	International Commission of Anglican–Orthodox Theological Dialogue
JB	The Jerusalem Bible
MISAG	Mission Issues and Strategy Advisory Group
NGO	Non-governmental Organisation (United Nations)
RSV	Revised Standard Version of the Bible
SPG	Society for the Propagation of the Gospel
UMCA	Universities' Mission to Central Africa
UN	United Nations
USPG	United Society for the Propagation of the Gospel
WCC	World Council of Churches

Member Churches
of the Anglican Consultative Council

The Anglican Church of Australia
The Church of Bangladesh
The Episcopal Church of Brazil (Igreja Episcopal do Brasil)
The Church of the Province of Burundi, Rwanda and Zaire
The Anglican Church of Canada
The Church of the Province of Central Africa
The Church of Ceylon (Sri Lanka)
The Council of the Churches of East Asia
The Church of England
The Church of the Province of the Indian Ocean
The Church of Ireland
The Holy Catholic Church in Japan (Nippon Sei Ko Kai)
The Episcopal Church in Jerusalem and the Middle East
The Church of the Province of Kenya
The Church of the Province of Melanesia
The Church of the Province of Myanmar (Burma)
The Church of the Province of New Zealand
The Church of the Province of Nigeria
The Church of North India
The Church of Pakistan
The Anglican Church of Papua New Guinea
The Philippine Episcopal Church
The Scottish Episcopal Church
The Church of the Province of Southern Africa
The Anglican Church of the Southern Cone of South America (Iglesia
    Anglicana del Cono Sur de América)
The Church of South India
The Church of the Province of the Sudan
The Church of the Province of Tanzania
The Church of the Province of Uganda
The Episcopal Church in the United States of America
The Church in Wales
The Church of the Province of West Africa
The Church in the Province of the West Indies

The motif which forms the visual focus of the cover design (by the Revd Drummond Chapman of the Church in Wales) is based on the Penarthur cross-slab in St David's Cathedral. The same cross provided the principal design element of a striking backcloth hanging behind the dais at the plenary discussions and corporate worship of ACC-8. The cross is one of a number of ninth or tenth century fretted ring-cross slabs found in the locality of St David's. It takes its name from Penarthur farm, where it was discovered more than a hundred years ago, and was believed to have been part of the masonry enclosing a holy well.

A World of Care

Participants in the eighth meeting of the Anglican Consultative Council (ACC) arrived on 21 July at Dyffryn House, near Cardiff in Wales, in brilliant sunshine and unexpected warmth, but they had not come to Britain to take part in holiday pursuits. From the very first moments of their meeting, violent and disturbing events in the wider world threw shadows of alarm and tragedy upon their discussions. The Church cannot ever distance itself from the world in which it ministers, but rarely can a council representing the great breadth of the Anglican Communion have been made so vividly aware of the universal challenges to its peace presented by secular pressures of a political, military, social, moral or environmental kind.

The Standing Committee of the ACC had convened according to plan two days earlier, in order to approve its own report to the Council and prepare the approach to a wide and demanding agenda. An empty chair at the committee table pointed eloquently to the absence of the Most Revd George Browne, Archbishop of West Africa. There could be no formal apology for absence. The news media told of the paralysis of Archbishop Browne's country Liberia, in the grip of a chaotic and bloody civil war, and a complete breakdown of communication and transport to the world outside; rumour added a report of the assassination of the archbishop at his home near the capital, round which the fighting was concentrated, but pleas for denial or confirmation were met with silence. In such a situation the essential nature of the Anglican Communion as a family asserts itself, a family that prays together, and when appropriate mourns or rejoices or acts together.

ACC-8 AND ITS AGENDA

So it was very much as a family that the members of the ACC, 63 in all representing 33 Churches or Provinces, together with their officers, met under the presidency of the Archbishop of Canterbury, the Most Revd Robert Runcie, and the chairmanship of the Venerable Yong Ping Chung, Bishop-elect of Sabah, from 22 July to 3 August 1990. This was the first occasion on which the important United Churches of the Indian sub-continent—the Church of Bangladesh, the Church of North India, the Church of Pakistan and the Church of South

India—took part in a meeting of the Council as full members. The assembled representatives were joined by two distinguished consultants who delivered special papers reproduced in this book on pages 51-85, by participants from two Churches in full communion, the Old Catholic and Mar Thoma Churches, and by representatives of the Lutheran World Federation, the Roman Catholic Church, the World Alliance of Reformed Churches and the World Council of Churches. The conference was supported by staff from the ACC secretariat and others seconded from various Churches of the Communion, and served by a chaplaincy team provided by the Church in Wales. A full list of all those present appears as Appendix III on pages 180-184.

The activity of the conference embraced worship, Bible study, and the consideration of a range of issues of particular current concern to the Church. The practical problems in attending to an extensive and in some respects specialised agenda led to the division of the participants into Sections for the earlier stages of discussion, coming together in plenary session for general presentations, business matters and, towards the end of the meeting, in order to share the fruit of the sectional sessions and draw in the contributions and comment of the entire Council.

Each Section had before it a number of documents that dealt with topics within its special terms of reference, but there were a number of papers which were studied by the whole Council, in many cases both sectionally and in plenary session. The four Sections, whose reports, finalised after discussion and adoption by the whole Council, appear on pages 86-139 below, were asked to consider: I Spirituality and Justice; II Mission, Culture and Human Development; III Evangelism and Communication; IV Unity and Creation. 'Identity and authority in the Anglican Communion' was a topic on which papers had been put before all members, but the difficulty of considering this in the normal sectional/plenary way led the Sections to set up a special joint working group of members nominated by each Section, under the chairmanship of Archbishop Hambidge, and their report appears on pages 140-143.

WORSHIP AND BIBLE STUDY

Worship was to be a plenary activity at the heart of the Council's life; there was a daily celebration of the Eucharist before work began, and the Council gathered for Evening Prayer at the end of each afternoon. Orders of service prepared by the chaplaincy team of the host Church were enriched from a specially compiled Worship Book drawing on the particular treasures of Welsh spirituality as well as on the common traditions of the Anglican Communion. Leadership of the services was shared widely among participants and staff.

Of particular importance was the daily hour and a half of Bible study planned by the chaplaincy team on a pattern set and highly valued by the Lambeth Conference. These sessions took place in twelve groups each of about ten participants, in which members from the Sections were joined by staff. They considered a series of passages from Luke under the general title 'The Church—a community', focusing on the development of the Christian community in the context of society as a whole in New Testament times, and linking that with our perception of the Church in the wider community today. The studies thus formed an exceptionally relevant setting and preparation for the discussion of many of ACC-8's leading themes. Not only did they succeed in rooting the whole work of the meeting in a biblical context, but they also introduced a depth of fellowship and intensity of communication among the participants which could not have been achieved in any other way. The groups spent time in prayer together as well as in studying Scripture.

Reviewing the fruitful—and joyful—experience of the study groups, the chaplaincy team reported:

> We feel that the importance of the Bible study groups was to be found in the process at least as much as in the content: in the listening to and sharing each other's stories and hopes and fears, often having to listen hard and wait for one another as we struggled with the difficulties of language and culture. Members spoke of learning to respect those who thought differently from themselves, and to value their 'struggling with what the Lord is saying'. As one group leader said, the Bible study groups provided the model for the rest of the work in the meeting, affirming that it should all be done in the context of silence and of listening to one another and to God.

The first joint action of the Council was in fact an act of worship, the Eucharist celebrated by the Archbishop of Wales in Llandaff Cathedral on the feast of St Mary Magdalene. The Archbishop of Canterbury preached the sermon (see pages 21-24) and the service was seen live on television throughout the British Isles. Taking as his text the Fourth Gospel's account of the appearance of the risen Christ to Mary of Magdala, the Archbishop dwelt in his sermon on the healing power of personal relationships in the new world which presents itself through our union with Christ. It was an apt message to a Council that would be drawn ever closer together by awareness of external events.

THE OPENING PLENARY SESSION

Members emerged from the cathedral service into another gloriously sunny day, to enjoy a reception and luncheon at the Cardiff Civic Centre, by courtesy of the Lord Mayor and Council, who graciously gave permission for the use of their Council Chamber for the opening plenary session of ACC-8.

The near-tropical weather did not distract the Council's attention from the inaugural addresses given by the President and Chairman, and the Secretary General's Review (pages 24-50). The Archbishop of Canterbury compellingly developed the thread he had begun to spin in his sermon, by speaking of the relationships which characterise Anglicanism—affection and communion—and how it draws strength from these while still valuing its diversity and the autonomy of its Provinces and Dioceses. The diversity of the Communion lends strength to its relations with other Christian Churches; noting the presence of the United Churches for the first time as full members, the Archbishop spoke of the Anglican Church's capacity to act as a bridge between divergent branches of the faith, as for example between the Roman Catholics and evangelical Protestant sects in Latin America. But diversity and autonomy in its various parts can blur the Communion's identity, and it may be difficult to discern the operation of order and authority within its structures. ACC-8 was invited to carry further the reflection on these matters which had taken place at the Lambeth Conference 1988 and at the subsequent Primates' Meeting in Cyprus in 1989.

The Chairman's address was in part an expression of farewell and gratitude in anticipation of the end of his own 11-year association with the ACC. But he also called upon the Council to stress as the cornerstone of all its work (whether in considering the Decade of Evangelism or in working on the broader themes reflected in the titles given to the Sections) commitment to a new life in Jesus Christ. Archdeacon Yong referred to the support of prayers and goodwill for the Council's work from all sides of the Communion family, and read from a message of commendation sent by the President of the USA.

The Secretary General, the Revd Canon Samuel Van Culin, in reviewing the tasks in front of the members of ACC-8, pointed out that this meeting, while reflecting upon the achievements of the Lambeth Conference of 1988, should bear in mind its responsibility for helping to shape the agenda of the next meeting of the Lambeth bishops. He referred to the ACC's increasing capacity to use the technology and techniques of modern communication, especially through the Inter-Anglican Publishing Network and the Inter-

Anglican Information Network (IAIN). Canon Van Culin pointed to an important development for the Anglican Communion in the appointment of the Right Revd Sir Paul Reeves, on completion of his term as Governor General of New Zealand, as the ACC's representative at the United Nations, and concluded by paying tribute to the life and work of the late Canon Martin Mbwana, the ACC's Secretary for Mission and Social Issues, a much loved friend of those present, who had died in Dar es Salaam on 20 March 1990.

WORLD CONCERNS

By the time the Council divided into Sections to begin its more regular programme of work on Monday 23 July, there was still no news of Archbishop Browne, although there was some assurance that the

The Most Revd George Browne, Archbishop of West Africa, seen with the Most Revd Edmond Browning, Presiding Bishop of ECUSA, during a visit to the United States. (Episcopal News Service)

assassination story had simply been an unsubstantiated echo of an earlier and discredited report. But the news indicated that conditions in Liberia were growing worse, and prayers continued for the Archbishop, his family and the people of his troubled country. Archbishop Browne had been named as the Chairman of Section II of ACC-8, and that role was taken over at short notice by the Very Revd Walter Asbil of Canada.

Liberia had not been the only African country arousing concern in the ACC and the Anglican Churches generally. In Kenya the opposition to an increasingly autocratic government had grown in recent months, and widespread calls for the introduction of a multi-party democracy had been supported by church leaders. This led to strident attacks upon the bishops by government ministers, against a background of anti-government rioting. As ACC-8 opened, the Archbishop of Canterbury had sent a message of support to Archbishop Manasses Kuria and Bishop Henry Okullu, and there was some alarm when Bishop David Gitari failed to arrive in Cardiff by the beginning of the meeting. In the event his delay turned out to be due to travel difficulties, perhaps aggravated by his being viewed as a 'dangerous cleric', as the Bishop goodhumouredly observed.

The prayers of the Anglican family were also being offered on behalf of the Philippines, from which confirmed reports were now arriving about the serious earthquake of the previous week, in which more than 1,500 had died and many hundreds of thousands had been made homeless, with after-shocks still continuing. The Most Revd Richard Abellon, the first Prime Bishop of the newly autonomous Philippine Episcopal Church and a co-opted member of the Council, reported that the Episcopal congregations, which had suffered widely in the devastation, were prominent in the relief operations, the churches being used as distribution centres for clothing and medical supplies.

THE COUNCIL AT HOME

Dyffryn House, appropriately enough for a meeting of the ACC, was built as a family home in the 1890s by prosperous mine-owners. Not that it could be confused with the simple 'two-up, two-down' dwellings, occupied by the families of humble miners, that greyly terrace the sides of the coal-bearing valleys of South Wales where the former owners of Dyffryn made their money. But Dyffryn was built for living in, and its rooms were not constructed on a scale suitable for a grand occasion or a great assembly, even the relatively modest numbers of the ACC. The lofty proportions of its so-called Great Hall were designed to impress rather than accommodate. So, in order to house the full complement of the ACC and its staff, a large marquee (or big tent; the curious English word marquee gave difficulty to members from some parts of the Communion) was erected at one end of the house, beyond a gothick billiard room of oddly ecclesiastical atmosphere. It was in the marquee that daily worship and the plenary meetings of ACC-8 took place, the members seated in a semicircle in front of a raised dais. Behind the dais, on which the altar was placed for worship, hung a green backcloth embodying a striking red, white and gold Celtic cross, designed by the Revd Drummond Chapman of the Church in Wales and based on the Penarthur Cross in the cathedral of St David's. Around the house and the marquee extended 55 acres of magnificent gardens, lovingly cared for by the Mid and South Glamorgan County Councils which now administer the house and grounds. Here in the midst of a collection of plants brought to Dyffryn from all over the world, members were able to feel at home, taking exercise, meditating, talking or simply relaxing in an environment apparently unpolluted by the dangers that figured prominently in the Council's discussions.

COMMUNION AND COMMUNICATION

While the Sections were still completing their preparatory work and finalising their own agendas, the full Council met twice to hear special papers delivered by Professor Jaci Maraschin of the Igreja Episcopal do Brasil and Bishop Roger Herft from the Church of the Province of New Zealand (pages 51-85), focusing on two important areas of the ACC-8 programme.

On a warm, humid evening, in the relatively open air of the marquee, Professor Maraschin offered provocative reflections on his theme of 'Growing in communion'. The crucial question for the Church was not numerical growth, he said, and went on to examine the roles of the institutions that Anglicanism has developed as the instruments of communion among its member Churches: the special position of the Archbishop of Canterbury, the Primates' Meeting and the Anglican Consultative Council. He saw these as the outcome, rather than the source, of the Church's communion. In the same way theological discourse is the product, not the producer of communion. It is our dependence on the working of the Holy Spirit, the love of God operating through the people of God, that enables growth in communion. Vividly illustrating his point with an account of the Archbishop of Canterbury and Cardinal Arns, at an ecumenical service in São Paulo, coming down from the high altar to be among the poorer people who thronged the nave, Professor Maraschin stressed

7

that it was necessary to look for growth in communion, not to the top of the institutional hierarchy or the heights of academic theological debate, but to 'theology by the people' at the grass roots, in which all could participate.

Bishop Herft's paper on 'The Gospel and communication' the following morning was likewise stimulating, not least in its exploitation of samples of auditory communication, which it is unhappily not possible to reproduce in this book. He looked at the potential dangers and inefficiencies in communicating the Gospel when communicator and receiver have different cultural backgrounds. God's central act of communication with humanity was through a unique medium: the Word made flesh. In apostolic times the act of evangelism was seen as God's task; the apostles simply allowed themselves to be the vessels of communication through witness, miracles, healing, martyrdom and other means. Traditionally Anglicans have not communicated well, and their task today is complicated by a new global, technological culture with which it can be difficult for the Church to make contact. Bishop Herft went on to offer extensive reflections on how Christians can fruitfully prepare to communicate the Gospel in the Decade of Evangelism.

A DISTURBED WORLD

While members were still digesting the practical lessons offered in Bishop Herft's address, news came of a terrorist bombing in Northern Ireland which claimed the lives of three policemen and a Roman Catholic nun. The attack took place in Armagh, the Diocese of Archbishop Robin Eames, Primate of All Ireland and a member of the Standing Committee of the ACC, which was temporarily deprived of his counsel while he returned to his Province to conduct yet another funeral, attending once more to this most unremitting of his pastoral cares.

Terrorism erupted in a different context a few days later, when members of the government of Trinidad including the prime minister were taken prisoner by a group of black Moslems, who also seized a government television station. An Anglican priest, the Revd Canon Knolly Clarke, was active as an intermediary in the negotiations for the release of the hostages. In the breakdown of law and order which accompanied this unrest, which had its root in the country's economic difficulties, Bishop Clive Abdullah made a radio appeal for an end to widespread looting.

Some participants were given a glimpse of another pastoral concern of the Church in a disturbed part of the world when the Vicar of Christ

Church, Bangkok, the Revd Monty Morris, paid a brief informal visit to Dyffryn House. He described hopes for a gradual revival of the Church's ministry in the countries of south-east Asia so long paralysed by political and economic chaos. He also spoke of the ministry of his own church to Karen refugees from Myanmar (Burma), some 20,000 of them, including a number of Christians, confined in an area just inside the borders of Thailand. The work had been supported by funds from the Church in Australia, New Zealand and the USA, and also by the Mothers' Union. The political situation was one of extreme delicacy; economic help to the refugees, among whom were students who had been in active opposition to the political regime in their own country and were now undergoing great deprivation, was virtually ruled out by the danger of attracting more refugees over the border and destabilising the situation still further.

A WORKSHOP ON AIDS

Not all the pastoral cares of the Church result from political or economic causes. Another visitor to ACC-8 was the Bishop of New Hampshire, the Right Revd Douglas Theuner, who came to Dyffryn House to lead a workshop on AIDS. Bishop Theuner is Chairman of the Joint Commission on AIDS of the Episcopal Church in the USA, which has devoted considerable energy and resources to a ministry to those who suffer from, are vulnerable to, and are engaged in the treatment of the HIV/AIDS virus, and is developing an impressive educational programme on the subject for young people. The Bishop, whose largely rural Diocese is not typical of the environment in which AIDS has been seen to flourish so far, emphasised that the pandemic was universal, like the Church, and 'like God, is no respecter of persons'. Recent figures published by the World Health Organisation estimated cases world-wide at 650,000, though that was two or three times the official count since, for a variety of reasons, concealment, falsification or miscalculation of statistics was common. AIDS is not, as had at one time been suggested, an African disease; 60 per cent of reported cases throughout the world were in the Americas, with the greatest concentration in the USA, the world's largest 'exporter' of the disease. The Church's healing ministry must be addressed to all without exception in the face of this pandemic, and must not be subject to any kind of moral quid pro quo. But it was true that the conditions in which AIDS was often transmitted were typically those against which the Church had directed its traditional moral teaching, and the present situation reinforced that teaching. The decade of AIDS would also be the Church's Decade of Evangelism, and this gave the opportunity to extend a message of Christian hope to counteract the prevailing climate of fear.

ACC members from Africa and Asia, particularly those from countries where a high level of infection was reported, responded warmly to Bishop Theuner's presentation, stressing the dangers of a 'scare' reaction. In Uganda, one of the earliest countries to recognise the size of the problem, the Church was reinforcing the government's programme of health education, as well as providing a ministry to victims and their families. In Tanzania panic reaction had shown itself in the churches by a fear of infection through receiving Holy Communion, and by a drop in the number of marriages. Governments might be afraid to talk about the disease in anticipation of an adverse effect on tourism, but the Church must act to prevent the development of a climate of fear. In Pakistan the officially reported cases numbered only three, but it was believed that the true size of the problem was far greater. No knowledge of the disease was available except through international news media; there was a need to explain the causes non-judgementally. The Church saw that it must make provision for AIDS in its caring and evangelistic ministry, but such was the level of ignorance that the impression had been given in that country that the Church wanted to give a licence to homosexual activity.

DISCOVERING WALES

In his Llandaff sermon the Archbishop had told members of ACC-8 that Wales required the stranger to discover its treasures. But the demands of agenda and timetable left them no time at all for exploration, beyond the cathedral and the city of Cardiff, and Dyffryn and its gardens. However, the efforts of the hosting committee chaired by Archbishop Noakes brought something at least of Wales into the experience of the visitors. Two evening entertainments were arranged, one at which they enjoyed traditional clog dancing, singing and harp music, and the other exciting them with the unique sound of a Welsh male voice choir from Risca. On occasion there was also the music of harp and voice to accompany the evening dinner.

On the Sunday in the middle of the conference one party of members travelled westwards past the industrial centres of the south coast and on through the beauty of West Wales in order to attend worship at the ancient cathedral of St David's, while another group saw something of the traditional coal-mining heart of South Wales on the way to Brecon Cathedral, and visited the picturesque Wye valley and the ruins of Tintern Abbey on the return journey.

COMMON THREADS

Despite the different subjects allocated for their consideration, the variety of documents used in their preparatory studies, and the diversity of their composition in terms of personalities and backgrounds, the four Sections of ACC-8 showed a notable convergence of themes and priorities in their respective reports. This may be less surprising when it is understood that deliberate overlaps were built into the assignment of subjects, so that a concept such as mission, for example, could be viewed from different perspectives. Even so, the degree of like-mindedness reflected a widespread common understanding of the present Anglican, and indeed Christian, agenda.

In every Section report there was stress on the importance of the individual, the local church and the local situation as the focus of attention for the Church's policies and activities. This is shown in Section I's identification of the personal aspect of spirituality, the individual's relationship with God, and of justice as having to do with interpersonal relationships. It is seen in Section II's endorsement of the findings of the World Convocation on Justice, Peace and the Integrity of Creation at Seoul, Korea, in March 1990, with their stress on human rights and individual freedom, as well as in the principle of local inculturation in liturgy. Section III emphasises person-to-person communication of the Gospel, the importance of telling personal stories, and caring for and valuing the individual in the evangelising local church, as more significant than handed-down institutional programmes; at the same time the Section draws attention to the dangers of the 'New Age' concentration on the self-centred development of the individual, rather than entering a personal relationship with Christ. Ecumenical activity, according to Section IV, has the greatest possibility of achieving lasting results at the local level, and the group considering Anglican identity and authority chose to resist concepts of authority 'from the top down'. This is of course consistent with the Archbishop of Canterbury's stress upon personal relationships and his reference to the kind of authority enjoyed by members of the Council as deriving from baptism, ordination and consecration rather than from Canon or Ordinance; also germane is Professor Maraschin's plea for communion with and among the people.

A key word in many debates was transformation. The definition of mission, whether in the broader context of the Church's prophetic role addressed by Section II or in the more specialised area of evangelism which was Section III's concern, inevitably involves the prospect of change, not only in the unjust structures of society but in the Church itself, in individual Christians and in those to whom the good news is made known. Transformation is implied in any consideration of justice in a world where injustice is widely manifest, and Resolution 3, arising from the work of Section I, pinpoints crisis areas where the Church must seek transformation of present conditions or attitudes.

There was universal concern about environmental problems. One might have expected that throughout the Judaeo-Christian tradition, with the figure of a Creator God and a creation narrative as the point of departure of its Scripture, the integrity of creation would be a dominant theme. The praise of God in creation has always been part of the expression of the Christian faith. But now, when the created world is seen to be under threat through the actions or neglect of its resident creatures, the mood has shifted from exultation to anxiety. This shows itself in Resolution 5, put forward to the Council by Section I, in the additional affirmation that Section II proposed to add to the four-fold definition of mission, and in the main thrust of Section IV's report, especially the 'Letter to our children'.

The expression of the Anglican sense of communion as a family relationship was a common feature of the attitudes demonstrated by ACC-8, but it would also be just to point to a growing consciousness of the wider Christian family, and a disposition to think within an ecumenical framework wherever possible. Section IV had before it 'The dodo report', prepared following the meeting of the Ecumenical Advisory Group in Mauritius in May 1990. Although the contents of this document are not reproduced as such in the Section's report, a number of its conclusions are translated into resolutions of ACC-8, notably the recommendation of Resolution 17 that future liturgical revisions of the Creed should omit the Filioque clause, removing a stumbling block in Anglican–Orthodox relations. It may be noted that Section I's discussions of spirituality dwelt upon Christian rather than specifically Anglican spirituality. Section II's commendation of the ecumenical Seoul document speaks for itself, and the linking of Anglican Liturgical Consultations with meetings of Societas Liturgica (Appendix II) demonstrates the increasingly ecumenical character of liturgical study. Following a recommendation of the Primates' Meeting in Cyprus, Section III took up a positive stance towards the involvement of other Christian denominations in the Decade of Evangelism, and noted a convergence between various Christian traditions in their current statements about the theology of mission.

Perhaps even more worthy of note is the general recognition of a need for dialogue with other faiths, which can be helpful, as Section III noted, in clarifying perception of some of the essentials of Christian truth. 'The dodo report' led Section IV to urge a sensitive approach to increasing dialogue with other religions, warning of the threat posed by the aggressive certainties of fundamentalism in all three world monotheistic faiths. Section I invited Christians to learn from the spiritualities of other faiths, even though they cannot be accepted as alternative paths to God.

LEADING THEMES

The common threads mentioned above indicate unifying features in the background to the work of the Sections, rather than the major themes of their separate discussions, which are the subject of formal reports printed on pp 86-143 below.

Section I, who had considered as part of their preparatory work the essays in C. Craston (ed.), *Open to the Spirit: Anglicans and the experience of renewal* (1987), and the 'Report of the Anglican Communion pastoral visit to Namibia, September 10-22, 1989', explored the relationship of Christian spirituality and justice in the light of both Scripture and their own experience as Christian people. Living justly is the working out in daily life of the true relationship of the believer with God. This has implications, not only for the human individual, but also for the Christian community, the Church, which must use its prophetic role to speak on behalf of the weak, the voiceless, the poor and the oppressed. Prayer and action are not optional alternatives for the Christian; Jesus is the model, in whom prayer and social action, but always in trustful obedience to the Father, are united.

Section II's preparatory studies had included 'Not by a committee', a review of the Partners in Mission consultations over the period 1976-89 prepared by the Revd Canon Geoffrey Cates. But they found themselves increasingly drawn into a consideration of the threats presented by the current global ecological crisis, and recognised that the Church's mission must include action aimed at preserving the integrity of creation. The findings of the Seoul Convocation offered a basis, and the Section called upon the Anglican Communion to respond positively to the Seoul programme. The other principal aspect of the Section's work was in relation to liturgy, and particularly the results of the third International Anglican Liturgical Consultation (ALC) of August 1989. The Section laid stress on the relationship of liturgy to life, especially in its function as a model of the Kingdom of God. With this in mind, the view of the ALC, following the Lambeth Conference of 1988, that liturgy should be in harmony with the cultural context in which it is used, assumed special importance. The Section offers in a supplement to its report illustrative samples of liturgical material, prepared within the framework of its own discussions, as a stimulus to local churches in their own explorations of liturgical composition.

The work of Section III was done with special reference to the Decade of Evangelism, and was focused around the report of the Mission Issues and Strategy Advisory Group (MISAG-2) 'Renew our vision in mission', incorporating a statement from the 1989 Primates' Meeting in Cyprus. Stressing that the essential need was for local churches to establish their own strategies and plans for implementing the Decade, the Section identified a number of aspects for general consideration, and suggested questions for each church to ask itself as a means of providing guidelines in its particular work of evangelism. Of major importance is the need to engage the skills and enthusiasm of the laity, and where appropriate to provide training for them. A general overview of the preparations and support for the Decade of Evangelism is given in the Section's report.

Respect for creation as the gift of God was a preoccupation of Section IV, as it was of Section II from a slightly different perspective. The expression of the Section's concerns in a 'Letter to our children' provided a practical resource, of which use will undoubtedly be made by local churches throughout the Communion, and the Section provided guidelines for doing this effectively. Ecumenical progress is now seen against the wider background of the integrity of creation, and correspondingly less emphasis is placed upon structural unity between the Churches. Nevertheless progress continues to be made in the traditional areas of ecumenical endeavour, including the World Council of Churches and the national and regional councils, while inter-Church co-operation at the local level is seen to be of fundamental importance. The Section report refers to the ongoing formal conversations between the Communion and other Churches. Special attention was given by the Section to the future of the Anglican Centre in Rome, its management and funding, and this became the subject of Resolution 18.

In the limited time at its disposal, the special group considering identity and authority in the Anglican Communion was only able to arrive at an interim view of the issues raised by the documents placed before it, and called for a more careful study, including attention to the underlying theology.

Readers of this report of ACC-8 may be surprised to find little attention to current divisions within the Church in relation to the ministry of women, especially at the meeting of the Council which followed the consecration of women as bishops for the first time by

The Right Revd Penelope Jamieson, the first woman to become an Anglican diocesan, was consecrated Bishop of Dunedin, New Zealand, on 29 June 1990. Among the participating bishops was the Right Revd Barbara Harris of ECUSA. (Episcopal News Service)

two member Churches. Resolution 27 welcoming the Eames Report was adopted after a short debate, in which divergent views on the question of women in the episcopate were voiced; it seemed properly to convey the mind of the Church at a time of study and reflection, and accurately expressed the intentions of all member Churches to maintain as high a degree of communion as possible.

THE CANTERBURY SUCCESSION

An unprogrammed event of special importance to the ACC took place at 11 a.m. on Wednesday 25 July, when the President announced to members of the Council the appointment of the Right Revd George Carey, Bishop of Bath and Wells, to succeed him as 103rd Archbishop of Canterbury in 1991. Expressing his pleasure and satisfaction at the choice, Dr Runcie passed on to the Council a message of greeting from Dr Carey. In a public statement he added:

> George Carey is a teacher and theologian particularly qualified to lead the Church in a Decade of Evangelism. He has quickly won all-round support in his Diocese. He commands respect and affection among us all in the House of Bishops. His broad sympathies have prepared him for the major part he plays in our Church's ecumenical relations. My prayers will be with him and his family as he prepares for his new responsibilities in God's Church.

THE COST OF COMMUNION

Not least among the problems of a world-wide fellowship of Churches is the cost of maintaining the links and services which provide the outward evidence of its strength. The President and Chairman both referred to the budgetary problems of the Inter-Anglican Finance Committee in their introductory addresses, and the important report of this Committee (pp 144-156) spelled them out in unmistakable terms. At a time of financial stringency for many member Churches, the need for increased contributions to central bodies which serve them all is a matter of deep concern. Yet what can be expected, if the Churches do not succeed in funding future inter-Anglican activities, is all too plain to see in the deferment of much needed ACC staff appointments, the cut in grant to (and prospective end to the funding of) the Anglican Centre in Rome, the shelving of the Theological and Doctrinal Commission, the postponement of meetings of ACC and the Primates, and a question mark even over the future of the Lambeth Conference. And these are simply responses to known deficits, with little regard to what may be to come.

CONGRATULATIONS, FAREWELLS, THANKS

One of the tasks of ACC-8 was to elect officers to succeed the Council's Chairman and Vice-Chairman, both due to retire after this meeting, and to replenish the membership of its Standing Committee, where vacancies arose because of the ending of members' terms of appointment. The Council was piloted through the unexpectedly intricate labyrinth of constitutional election procedure by the unfailing patience and good humour of Archbishop Eames, the Chairman of the Nominations Committee, and arrived at a pleasing result in the choice of the Revd Canon Colin Craston (England) as Chairman and the Revd Canon Simon Chiwanga (Tanzania) as Vice-Chairman. Canon Craston's long service to the ACC has included six years as Vice-Chairman of the Council and the vice-chairmanship of the Inter-Anglican Finance Committee. The new members of the Standing Committee were Mrs Betty Govinden (Southern Africa), the Most Revd Douglas Hambidge (Canada) and the Right Revd Alexander Malik (Pakistan).

The Standing Committee had already addressed themselves to the position of Secretary General, in view of the ending of the Revd Canon Samuel Van Culin's present appointment in 1992. To the great satisfaction of members, they invited him to remain in office until 1994, beyond the prospective date of the meeting of ACC-9.

In the closing stages of ACC-8, the Council were obliged reluctantly but with great warmth and affection to say goodbye to their current Chairman and President. The evening before the final session, the Revd Tevita Talanoa of Papua New Guinea presented Archdeacon Yong with symbolic gifts from his Province. Music was an essential part of such a presentation, he said, and performed to his own guitar accompaniment a traditional farewell song addressed to someone about to embark on a new phase of his life, in Yong Ping Chung's case as Bishop of Sabah. (Tevita Talanoa confessed to fellow members of his Bible study group that he had once been a night-club singer.)

After completing the passage of the formal resolutions arising from the Council's work (see pp 157-171), the final plenary session adopted special resolutions of thanks to the Venerable Yong Ping Chung and the Archbishop of Canterbury, attending their last meetings as, respectively, Chairman and President of ACC.

As a tangible remembrance of his eleven years of association with the Council and six years as its Chairman, Bishop-elect Yong was presented with a pastoral staff, the gift of members and staff of the ACC. Expressing his thanks and pleasure, Yong Ping Chung said that he would like to be thought of as a servant bishop, and asked for the support of the prayers of all his friends at ACC-8.

As the retiring Chairman emphasized, the mere passing of a resolution was not enough to mark the end of Archbishop Runcie's presidency, and he invited a number of members of ACC to pay tributes which would be shared by all.

Bishop Sumio Takatsu's only recollection of his first meeting with Dr Runcie was a conversation about Italian food; sublimely memorable, however, was the Archbishop's recent visit to Brazil when he was greeted by the Roman Catholic Cardinal in São Paulo and the people as 'Robert Runcie, messenger of God, apostle of peace, friend of the poor and defender of human rights.' According to Archbishop Donald Robinson, no visiting archbishop had ever endeared himself so quickly to the Church in Australia, a Province which had received him twice during his primacy; all parts of the Anglican Communion recognised that Archbishop Runcie had shown a quite remarkable degree of leadership in a very difficult time. The privilege of having been present at his installation was recalled by Bishop David Gitari, who referred enthusiastically to the encouragement he personally had derived from Dr Runcie's prophetic ministry, his readiness to challenge the world's secular powers, and at the same time to be all things to all men and women, as shown in his comprehensive personal concern for members of the ACC. The sense of personal relationship at a 'family' level was also evoked by Mrs Betty Govinden of Southern Africa, who recalled with particular appreciation the comfort the Archbishop's friendliness gave in the special atmosphere of the Lambeth Conference. Bishop Sigisbert Kraft voiced the Old Catholic Churches' perception of Dr Runcie as a helpful guide, a spiritual leader, a faithful preacher of the Gospel, a good friend and a father in God.

Bishop Alexander Malik spoke of the universal regard for the Archbishop extending beyond the Christian community; in Pakistan even the Moslems had appreciated him. Bishop James Ottley's tribute focused on the way in which Dr Runcie's incumbency had made the office and person of the Archbishop of Canterbury become real to the people of Latin America. His personal touch, the time and trouble he took to know and understand, the evidence of love and concern for the powerless and voiceless, had led very many to thank God for his leadership, sense of mission and witness to the world on behalf of the Anglican Communion. Bishop Samuel Ebo spoke of the honour in which Archbishop Runcie was held in Nigeria, the country with the largest Anglican population in the Communion, as an inspired enabler, a wise administrator, a humble leader and a trustworthy shepherd. A typical anecdote formed part of Bishop Edmond Browning's contribution. It had been arranged that Dr Runcie should visit a poor quarter in the course of a visit to Hawaii. In view of a hepatitis epidemic, attempts were made to cancel the walkabout, but the Archbishop insisted it should go ahead. As the visitors entered one house an agitated aide whispered, 'Don't go too close; they might sneeze.' The Archbishop went in and sat down at once, close to an indistinct figure on a small bench. 'I'm Robert,' he announced. 'What's your name?' A bishop of the people, and a friend of the people, Bishop Browning called him. 'No one', he told Dr Runcie, 'has given a greater sense of unity to our ministry. If anyone deserves the title Your Grace, you do.'

The Chairman mentioned with disdain, as several previous speakers had done, offensive references to the Archbishop of Canterbury which had appeared in some sections of the British press. The ACC and the Anglican Communion at large took a very different view. Whenever Archdeacon Yong spoke to real people about Dr Runcie the reaction was always one of unhesitating warmth. His love and care, gentleness and generosity reflected the light of Christ. Churches had been encouraged, challenged, inspired and strengthened by his visits. He had dared to make a stand when needed, and to take risks on behalf of the Church. 'God raised up a leader after his own heart,' said Archdeacon Yong, 'and gave that leader to us.'

Returning thanks for a deeply affectionate succession of tributes, the President recalled asking his predecessor Archbishop Coggan what one should be doing when listening to speeches like this. 'You should be praying,' answered Lord Coggan severely. 'Praying for yourself because you're enjoying it so much. And praying for the others who are telling such awful lies.' Dr Runcie spoke of his time as Archbishop of Canterbury and President of the ACC as an extended love affair with the Anglican Communion. Summing up what the experience had meant to him, he said, 'I am a firmer believer now than when I began to be Archbishop of Canterbury, because I have seen Christ at work.'

Finally, special expressions of thanks and farewell were made to the Church in Wales, the Hosting Committee, the chaplaincy team and Archbishop George Noakes, whom Dr Runcie characterised as 'someone who lets good things happen, that couldn't happen if he wasn't there.'

THE MESSAGE OF ACC-8

And what did ACC-8 achieve? To expect dramatic initiatives and spectacular effects may be futile when the world is in a condition of accelerating change, its lines of communication becoming ever shorter and its problems ever more interwoven. Certainly the Church has become more aware that it must be able to react prayerfully and pragmatically to an infinite variety of local situations, in loving obedience to God and fortified by the collective wisdom and diverse experience of the community of faith.

The world makes no concessions. As ACC-8 dispersed, external crises still cast their shadows, some darker, some changed in shape, some completely new. From Liberia there had still been no news of Archbishop Browne, but a horrific massacre of 200 civilians by troops in the grounds of a Lutheran church had been reported, and international initiatives to re-establish peace had made no progress. Further stories of abuse of the environment continued to sting authorities into recrimination rather than action. More ominous and immediate, a major military build-up of Iraqi forces was taking place on the borders of Kuwait.

Members of the Council prepared to return to their home Churches having gained new strength to carry out the mission in which they share, and in so doing, deepening a communion which exists not so much by virtue of external structures as through a common acknowledgement of what the Lord requires: 'to act justly, to love tenderly, and to walk humbly with your God'.

But there was something more. One of the ACC-8 Bible studies entitled 'Called to Mission' explored Luke 9.1-10, the sending of the Twelve by Jesus to proclaim the Kingdom of God and to heal. Throughout their discussions the members of ACC-8 came to see these two goals as paramount and indissolubly linked. Time and again the broken nature of our world is expressed in the metaphors of disease and decay. Some of its symptoms, it is true, are clinical conditions—like AIDS and the injuries inflicted by terrorism and violence—which may in time yield to medical procedures. But it is chiefly to underlying spiritual causes that the Church must direct its healing mission.

In stating its concern for creation as a whole, ACC-8 set an agenda for the transformation of our society and the life and role of the Church. It has shown how Christian spirituality must provide the ground in which we are to root concepts of justice which challenge the existing order on behalf of the weak, the voiceless, the poor and the oppressed, whether they are the victims of unjust social, cultural, economic or political structures. The Council called for due weight to be given to the claims and protection of the individual and of local culture, in societies dominated by institutions, ideologies and secular authorities. It laid stress on the unity of creation and of humanity within it, and on the right and duty of us all, irrespective of race or creed, together to preserve for our children God's gift of our environment against the destructive forces which already significantly corrupt it. All this will mean fundamental change in the attitudes, structures and practices of the Church itself. But nothing of this programme can be achieved unless it is led and undergirded by that other goal of the Church's mission: the proclamation of the Kingdom of God through the person of the Lord Jesus Christ.

THE EDITOR

Introductory Addresses

SERMON

BY THE ARCHBISHOP OF CANTERBURY

Delivered on Sunday 22 July 1990 in Llandaff Cathedral at the opening of the eighth meeting of the Anglican Consultative Council.

> Jesus said to her, 'Mary'. She turned and said to him in Hebrew, 'Rabboni', that is to say 'Master'. (John 20.16)

It is no exaggeration to say that the world has come to Llandaff this morning—represented by Christians of many nations, races and languages. And we have all heard the story of the appearance of the Risen Christ to Mary Magdalene.

It is a story of simplicity, wonder and respect: no fanfare of trumpets or public announcement. The first appearance of the Risen Christ was private and personal. It is the same in the other Easter stories: a garden, an upper room, an empty road, a lake shore. In each case the identity of the Risen Christ is first hidden from those he meets. He is mistaken for someone else: a gardener, a stranger on the lake shore, an ill-informed visitor to Jerusalem. The wonder of God's power is revealed in the ordinary places and people of day-to-day life.

Jesus calls Mary by name and she replies in Hebrew, a perfect example of communication. Recognition passes between them, understanding is established, friendship restored.

A Council of the Anglican Communion devoted to consultation needs to ponder this story. We need to appreciate the real language of the Gospel: simplicity, respect, forgiveness, friendship. These are the ways Jesus makes himself known. We have come to consult one another, but like any Christian assembly we cannot start talking until, like Mary in the garden, we have turned to Jesus and discovered him standing among us. That is at the heart of our religion. So we gather beneath the majestic figure of Christ standing on a bridge, and we turn to Christ in worship and adoration. Each day of our meeting we shall do the same.

But we come also to listen: to listen to each other, and so to God.

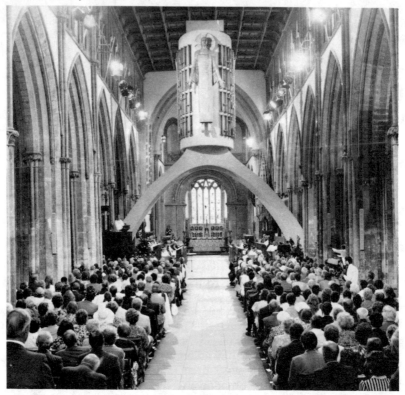

The Archbishop of Canterbury, 'beneath the majestic figure of Christ standing on a bridge,' preaches to ACC-8 in Llandaff Cathedral.

We shall find that whatever our language, God will address us in terms as unmistakable as the words he used to Mary in the Easter garden. He calls us all by name.

There is a story of a Welsh girl who came to London to work as a maid for a wealthy family. She lived with them, and she attended a Welsh church and travelled many miles across London to worship in the language she loved. One day the master of the house invited her to worship at the local parish church with the rest of the family. She politely declined, and he said to her in a kindly way, 'You know, Jesus was not a Welshman.' 'I know that, sir,' she said, 'but it is in Welsh he speaks to me.'

Such has been the experience of the Christian Church since the first Pentecost. God speaks to us in our own language.

Anglicanism places great value on the distinctiveness of each nation and culture. We all belong to a local Province or national Church. We rejoice in our diversity. We wish to appreciate each other and to understand one another's gifts and customs, traditions and institutions, not that we may demonstrate the superiority of our own, but so that we may see anew the generosity and creativity of God.

Such fellowship can be distorted when conviction hardens into domination, or if respect degenerates into submission. It is always threatened by disagreement. So it has always been, even among the first disciples. There was impulsive Peter and reflective John, silent Mary and questioning Thomas, Nathanael from the country and Matthew from the city. Who can imagine that they were free of tension?

St Paul tells us, 'When anyone is united to Christ, there is a new world' (2 Cor 5.17). We find that easy to believe about the first disciples. It is more difficult to understand for ourselves, conscious as we are of our own failures and shortcomings. How can we bring about a new world?

St Paul believed that the sign of new life in Christ was renewal in relationships with each other. Mary Magdalene, previously disordered in her thinking and disordered in her way of life, had been healed. A sign of being healed is the new quality of relationships a person has with other people. St Paul took it for granted that a new and better world begins with new and better personal relationships. Could he be right?

For the last century public opinion has been against him. Public opinion has been that the defects and problems of our world can be remedied and solved only by expertise—only by the skill and knowledge of economists, sociologists, political analysts, international negotiators with a multitude of facts and figures at their fingertips. Public opinion has been that the way the world is depends on the intellectual skill and expertise of each powerful person who manages it.

Suddenly the climate has begun to change. The personal relationships of the world's leaders have been seen to become a bit more trusting. Problems which have beset us for decades are now solved in days. The will of some world leaders to work together, their new sensitivity to one another's difficulties, their new disposition to understand rather than defeat those who disagree with them: this new spirit offers real hope that a better era will dawn, a better order for the world and its people.

There is a message here for this Council. You come from many different countries and cultures, from Anglican Churches of very different character. You must be true to the places you represent. But you will do so more effectively in proportion to the way in which personal relationships in this Council are mutually respectful, understanding and, if I may use the word, affectionate. May this Eucharist on St Mary Magdalene's day sustain, or renew, or create amongst us the quality of personal relationships which heal and redeem humanity.

We celebrate this Eucharist in the ancient and beautiful cathedral which graces the capital city of Wales. Wales is a land of many secrets. The wealth of its history and culture is to be found in churches of great antiquity standing on lonely headlands or tiny offshore islands; it is to be found in deep valleys where human existence depended so long on hidden, underground resources of lead, copper and coal; in a language which, to the stranger, is like no other; in a quality of choral music which astounds the visitor when unexpectedly it is heard emerging from chapel or village hall. Wales does not parade or advertise its treasures. It requires the stranger to discover them.

And is that not true of our relationships as well? We must discover one another before we can respect and value one other. That is what some world leaders have been discovering in the past two years. I pray that it will characterise the meeting of this Council. We shall discover the variety, the differences and diversity which exist amongst us— signs not of the absence of the Spirit, but of the generosity of God's gifts. He speaks to us individually by name and in our own language, but he goes on to call us to life together, and it is in union with Christ we know his will can be done together.

Sometimes I have heard a speaker say on the eve of a conference such as this, 'Do not expect too much.' I say to you this morning, 'Do not expect too little.' For 'when anyone is united to Christ, there is a new world; the old order has gone and a new order has already begun'.

PRESIDENTIAL ADDRESS

By the Archbishop of Canterbury on Sunday 22 July 1990 in Cardiff City Council Chamber at the opening of the eighth meeting of the Anglican Consultative Council.

When, in the sixth century, my predecessor St Augustine met the Welsh bishops, he did not show them proper respect. The Welsh party had been instructed by a wise hermit that if the Archbishop of

Canterbury rose from his seat and greeted them, then 'you will know that he is a servant of Christ and you should listen to him obediently. But if he despises you and is not willing to rise in your presence, you should despise him in return.' I'm afraid Augustine remained seated. The historian Bede wrote: 'When they saw this, they forthwith became enraged and, setting him down as a proud man, strove to contradict everything he said.'

My predecessor's lack of humility resulted in four centuries of dispute between Wales and Canterbury. Even then, unity was only achieved by the subjection of the Welsh dioceses to Canterbury, an injustice only put right by the re-creation of the Welsh Province in 1920.

This story is a good reference point for us as we think, talk and pray about the identity and authority of the Anglican Communion. None of us must sit arrogantly in the presence of others; if we do, the cost to our unity may have to be calculated in terms of centuries rather than decades.

In this address I want to talk about three features of Anglicanism: its capacity to use *affection and friendship* creatively; its ability to value *diversity*; and its difficulty in maintaining *communion* without abandoning the principle of *autonomy*.

These themes are not new. And they are not exclusively Anglican issues. They are found in the pages of the New Testament. The early Church discovered them in the first years of its existence. They remain part of the dynamic of Christian life. A scholar recently in my presence described church history as largely the story of the quarrels of good men and women. What characterises Anglicans is the way we deal with them. In some areas I think we are on the right track, but a body like the ACC must not be afraid to face the most difficult questions for the benefit of the Church as a whole.

Let me begin with an unqualified positive thought. It is this: between Provinces, as between individual Christians, simple friendship and mutual care are an essential element of our fellowship in the Gospel.

Internationally we carry one another's burdens by programmes of partnership, by understanding each other's different circumstances, by mutual care for each other. Without them, our Communion is just as surely impaired as it is by any lack of doctrinal agreement.

A Church that is isolated, cut off, oppressed, restricted needs its communion with the world-wide Anglican family to be expressed in visible and concrete ways: by personal visits, by exchange of ministries, by sharing of gifts, by inclusion and recognition at international gatherings such as this Council. This, as well as agreement on orders, is part of what communion means.

Inevitably the weaker look to the stronger, the smaller look to the larger, the oppressed look to those who are free. Yet when contact is made in these ways, it is not at all clear who is the stronger or who is the more free. Suffering can sharpen witness and deepen faith.

Someone once said to me of a popular priest: 'He's very nice and good, but somehow I don't think he's suffered much.' There are some who say that about my own Church.

So I am always pleased when I hear of journeys of support and programmes of partnership between Provinces, schemes that strengthen communion between us. I am grateful for the generosity of people like you who often make it possible. There was the visit of the Primates of the West Indies, Canada and the United States to the Church in Nicaragua and Panama last year. There was the group I sent to Namibia last September at a time of critical importance for the future of Southern Africa. Archbishop Ted Scott of Canada led it— that gives me hope for life after retirement—and there was a bishop from Western Australia, a lawyer from Zimbabwe, a layman from the United States, and two laywomen, from the Province of the Middle East and from England. The group went to demonstrate our support for Anglicans in that Diocese and to tell the world that we are a Christian family who care for each other. It meant a lot to my friend James Kauluma.

I recall the day when he was in exile and we consecrated him Bishop for Namibia in Westminster Abbey. What a lot of friendships were created on that day!

You will know that the Archbishop of Canterbury is often described—inaccurately—as the head of the Anglican Communion. Indeed, in some countries the fact I have no grander title than Archbishop causes problems. In one place I was 'the Lord High Primate'—which sounds like a monkey in a tree-top.

It is not only the media which find it easier to concentrate on a person than on a committee, especially when that person lives in a sophisticated modern capital at the centre of a diplomatic network and efficient communications. But I do not rule. I serve the Communion, not only by crisis management, but by gathering it and sometimes speaking for it. I am only a senior bishop with a Diocese like other bishops. I believe that should remain the case. When it comes to nominating my successor, a large proportion of the vote will come from my Diocese. Yet I have the enormous privilege of knowing how much this partnership we enjoy as a Communion in our sort of world can mean—from my own observations and from my daily postbag.

I recently received a letter from the Archbishop of Burma, Andrew Mya Han. He made a great impression on us at the Lambeth Conference. He is someone whose simplicity and buoyancy of faith contrast strongly with the conditions he describes at home. He told me how the price of rice had more than doubled in the previous few months, and how many people have no regular meals. But he told, too, of new mission work in his Diocese of Rangoon and Mandalay. 'We carry out our programmes without transport, medicine or lights. I take pride as an Anglican and praise God for choosing me to lead this part of our work.' Archbishop Andrew Mya Han and his Church need all our support. And here today we think particularly of Archbishop George Browne, a valued member of this Council, in a time of great tragedy in his country Liberia, unable to reach us. I have sent a message to him, as I have to Bishop Henry Okullu and Archbishop Manasses Kuria in their difficulties in Kenya.

Of course I am aware always of the enormous world-wide support in prayer for all our efforts to remember and secure the return of Terry Waite and the hostages. One visible answer to the volume of prayer for him is the immense courage displayed by his wife and children, his redoubtable mother, brother and sister. One day I believe there will be further evidence of answers to our prayers for this man who played such a large part in introducing me to the ACC in Newcastle and Nigeria.

In February I was in Pakistan and Bangladesh, where the United Churches play a part on the international stage out of all proportion to their size. I believe that some secular leaders there are coming to see how religious plurality can enrich society, and that true holiness and true humanity can build bridges across traditional divides. In Islamabad I laid the foundation stone of a new church. Since there are mosques now in my country, I said it was only right that there should be a number of churches in their country. Not everything went smoothly. We were heckled by a persistent and hectoring mullah from a neighbouring minaret. Yet afterwards an Islamic scholar confessed, 'Clerical education of our mullahs has not advanced here as far as in other parts of the Muslim world'.

It is not for me to underestimate the devastating effects on the Church of the clash of religious fanatics. But my own experience of co-operation with British Muslim leaders has revealed how there can be dialogue and common action for human wellbeing, built on the basis of individual friendship. Some of you will feel the imperatives of this much wider than Christian ecumenism, even more keenly than we do in Britain.

I have talked of *affection:* now of our *diversity* in Christ.

The United Churches in Pakistan, Bangladesh and India are good examples of diversity. I welcome them for the first time as full members of this Council today. They enlarge the boundaries of our Communion. This reminds us that Anglicanism has never claimed to be more than part of the one holy catholic and apostolic Church. These United Churches and also the post-denominational Church in China are signals of our ecumenical vocation. Their bishops, including Bishop Ting, who has been in touch with me and knows about this meeting, want to share the life of our Communion, but not at the expense of their unity with other traditions. It is another example of what Desmond Tutu described as the untidy but very loveable Anglican Communion. We could make our Communion much more tidy, but it might be much less loveable, and we would be impoverished as a result.

In January I was in Ethiopia. There are scarcely any Ethiopian Anglicans, but our Communion is held in much honour in that ancient Christian and suffering country. This puzzled me, until I discovered that Anglican missionaries working in Ethiopia in decades long past directed all their converts to the Ethiopian Orthodox Church. The traditions of that historic Church could hardly be in starker contrast to the conservative evangelization of some of those missionaries. But they saw a deeper bond, and their way of being a missionary Church, but not a proselytising Church, has led to a trust of Anglicans in both aid and development work and in education which paper ecumenism could never achieve.

That example might be ecclesiologically untidy, but I can think of nothing more fundamental to building up the Body of Christ. Our untidiness is potentially creative. It may be that the time has come to concentrate less on increasing refinement and more on the preservation of variety in theology. Our friends in the Green movement remind us that in the natural world we have learned of the importance of preserving variety in species. I believe there is a similar need in theology. Truth is many-sided. Only a Church which can comprehend diversity can believe in the development and unfolding of God's truth.

In the last 400 years some dogmatic theology, Roman, Orthodox and Protestant, has concentrated on the suppression of other opinions and the replacing of them by a single 'correct' variety. Theological systems have, like capitalism and science-based technology, proved immensely effective, but their achievements have sometimes been bought at a high cost to the freedom of the human spirit.

As the Anglican Communion we need to reaffirm our tradition of unity in diversity, our commitment to comprehensiveness. Tradition is not to be thought of as a package without loose ends. It is, in Newman's phrase, 'an ever-widening stream'.

This variety does make it still possible for us to be seen as a Church that can bring others together. Nowhere has this been better demonstrated to me than in my recent experience in Latin America. In these countries the Catholic hierarchy, whether conservative or radical, is consistently suspicious of Pentecostal and evangelical sects. Those groups in turn lace their enthusiasm with a good deal of anti-Catholic rhetoric. Often I found myself speaking to meetings arranged for me at which cardinals and Pentecostal leaders either met each other for the first time, or discovered that they had more in common than their rhetoric recognised. The Anglican Church—a small Church in South America—proved its capacity to act as a bridge between divergent forms of Christianity.

In this year of revolutions in Europe the Churches have often played a dramatic part. I hope there may be an opportunity for me to pursue this matter later at this meeting. Gatherings in Basel and Geneva have been the most representative of all Christian traditions for a thousand years. Anglicans have had a place in both. Though we are largely confined to these islands, and only found in scattered communities elsewhere in Europe, we must be seen and see ourselves as a European Church. The other European Churches are our natural partners, I believe, in the evangelism of this secularised continent. There is sometimes, can you believe it, suspicion that the English city of Canterbury is a relic of colonial Britain. But Canterbury should increasingly be seen, as it has always been, as a European city. The Anglican Communion may not need England, but it certainly needs a stake in Europe, the cradle of Christian humanism.

In Latin America I visited an Indian community in Paraguay. Christian humanism in Europe seemed a long way from their traditions. They were rooted in the study of the Scriptures. I sensed that my sermon was a bit weak on the Bible. It was Ascension Day. As I walked away with some of the pastors through the long grass I trod on a large snake. But it did not bite me. Everyone raised their hands in horror. 'Mark 16,' I said. 'It is part of the Ascension story: you shall pick up snakes and they will not kill you.' There was much delight. A Bible man after all!

Yet if we can be proud of our capacity for variety, I want now to issue some warnings. First, if our Communion is to win people to a personal faith in Jesus Christ, then we must strengthen those things which hold us together: teaching drawn always out of and tested by the Scriptures; the tradition of ordered worship which elevates and does not trivialise; the ability to share together in sacramental life which has its heart in the Eucharist. Throughout the world people look to the Church for firmness in faith, affirmation of moral standards and support of the weak and oppressed. They do not think they find it when there is no sense of authority or doctrinal confidence. We shall need this sort of authority for what we intend to do in our several ways for the Decade of Evangelism.

Furthermore, we have to acknowledge that other Christians find the Anglican Communion a puzzling partner in ecumenical relations. It is said that we need an ecumenical movement among ourselves. It is pointed out that the ordination of women, for example, may impair inter-Anglican relations more than some of our associations with other local Churches. The Anglican model of communion, some say, may look fine on paper, but in practice it cannot withstand the pressure of headstrong members who are determined to go it alone.

We have tried to meet these complaints in some measure by strengthening our bonds of consultation. The Lambeth Conference of bishops has proved itself to be more important than we thought. Who can deny that the 1988 Conference gave a great boost to morale in the Communion? The custom of Primates' Meetings enables a further degree of consultation and common decision-making. Now we meet in Wales at the eighth Anglican Consultative Council.

I believe we must address the awkward historical fact of our autonomy. But I don't think it should obsess us. Nor should we be led to believe ourselves impaired as a Church by this untidy feature of our structure.

St Paul, when developing the doctrine of the Body of Christ, emphasized the interdependence which characterises *koinonia* or communion. Ever a practical man, he expressed this not only in abstractions but in material ways too, most notably the collection for the saints which he organized. Few things are a greater test of communion than the financial cost, as those who wrestle with the ACC budget will know. Perhaps Romans 15.25-27 is a sign of how we should sort out that problem. St Paul writes:

> I am going to Jerusalem with aid for the saints. For Macedonia and Achaia have been pleased to make some contribution for the poor among the saints at Jerusalem; they were pleased to do it, and indeed they are in debt to them, for

if the Gentiles have come to share in their spiritual blessings,
they ought also to be of service to them in material blessings.

Paul makes the same point in 2 Corinthians 8.4 and 9.13.
Fellowship, communion, *koinonia* means doing something not just
with others, but *for* others. Communion is not rooted in bonhomie or
enjoying one another's company, but in a sense of mutual
dependence.

This is the key to understanding the distinctive gift of Christianity
to the world. Identity and unity are discovered when we live not for
ourselves, but for others and so for God. What is true for individual
Christians is true for the whole body, true for Churches. The New
Testament does not speak merely of living for others, but of 'dying to
live'.

Anglicanism betrays its character—and the Gospel—when it hangs
on to its identity at all costs. That is true of Provinces as well as of our
Communion as a whole.

So even our communion with one another is not an end in itself. It
exists only for the sake of the Gospel. We should remember that
agencies to strengthen communion are not diminished in importance
by that truth. The Council of Jerusalem was not rendered unnecessary
because there was a sense of the provisional about its decisions in the
light of the expected return of the Lord. There were matters to be
determined for the good of the whole body, to keep it alive for that
day.

You may think ACC-8 is a long way, in time and space if not
perhaps in spirit, from the Council of Jerusalem. How many
Anglicans know we are meeting here? Few, I expect. How many
Anglicans believe their discipleship will be affected by what we
decide? Even fewer, I daresay. How many Anglicans would reckon
this meeting a waste of resources? Probably rather a lot. We must face
those uncomfortable facts, and not believe our fellow Christians
unenlightened or lacking in vision for thinking them. We can only
overcome them by being of service to the Communion, not by making
the ACC an end in itself and suggesting it has an authority which
Anglicans generally are reluctant to give it.

Your place is to work at the issues I have raised and do some hard
thinking about them. The Church generally undervalues its thinkers.
But it depends upon them more than it knows. Newman once said that
one of the primary causes of corruption in the Church was 'obstinacy
in the notions of the past'. It is part of our interdependence in the
Body of Christ to be fed by the thinking and praying of others. We
don't always recognise or honour the sources of our nourishment.

It has been said that the ACC is not only a think-tank but a work-horse for the Anglican Communion. We should not be ashamed of that. It will only be of true service if strong opinions are expressed and conflicts sometimes surface. Here, as in earlier ACCs, a sense of our own communion, our interdependence, will grow. That is right and good and Christian. But that is not the reason we come together. Telling those who were not there what a wonderful sense of communion existed at the Lambeth Conference was true, but not always compelling for those who never experienced it, and had to pay the bill. Our task is to put the experience of others *first,* and think imaginatively of those in whose name we meet. That is one of the priorities of a synodical assembly—and the ACC is a remarkable attempt to give expression to the synodical character of our Provinces in a way which is unique amongst Christians of catholic order.

The creation of the ACC was our Communion's boldest attempt to match the need for coherence and order with the wide degree of freedom and autonomy our Provinces enjoy. But the creation of the ACC does not in itself answer the problem. It provides a vehicle for addressing issues, of which one of the most pressing is our difficulty in maintaining communion without abandoning the principle of autonomy.

Let me state the problem simply. Throughout the Provinces there are canonical and juridical arrangements which control the autonomy of the Diocese. Yet in the Communion as a whole there are no such canonical or juridical arrangements which control the autonomy of the Provinces. But there is an inherent authority experienced and expressed in two ways: in the whole people of God through baptism; and in the three-fold order of ministry through ordination.

With juridical questions unresolved, there may arise a tension between those two forms of authority—the first appearing to be represented here, the second more characteristic of the Lambeth Conference. I believe that at a time of rapid change we ought to have the courage to allow both the ACC and the Lambeth Conference to assume a synodical role when particular need arises. A resolution agreed by both bodies might then be accepted by the Communion as a whole, but by common consent rather than the rule of law. That would also do something to unite those two streams of inherent authority.

Both the authority of the people of God and the authority of the Episcopate exist prior to any particular juridical or canonical arrangements. These are always secondary. Canons and Laws and Constitutions and Declarations of Faith do not confer authority on people or bishops. They recognise and embody an already latent authority in view of baptism and ordination. So you, members of the ACC, are not here ultimately as delegates from sovereign national synods. Your inherent authority is by virtue of your baptism, ordination and consecration.

If we grasp this fundamental insight, we can begin to think much more creatively about our structures.

Once we get away from political models of delegation and representation, we can be much more flexible about bodies such as the Lambeth Conference, the Primates' Meeting and the ACC itself.

We have a model for this in the early Ecumenical Councils. Held to be authoritative, they were hardly representative. The bishops were, in the vast majority, from the eastern part of the Church. There were no laity, unless you count the Emperor, who actually convoked and in part presided. There were few priests, except those who acted as legates of the most powerful sees, such as Rome itself. So the Ecumenical Councils, which gave us the fundamental, scriptural doctrines of Jesus Christ and the Holy Trinity, fit no tidy theoretical pattern. In that respect they are very Anglican.

So why should not the Lambeth Conference, the ACC, or the Primates' Meeting be more flexible for what is required for the particular occasion—even an authoritative decision of faith or order for the whole Communion?

There will be times when it is right to bring together as many experiences of the local Church as possible. Here I think the bishops from all the Dioceses in a Lambeth-type conference is the right model. But if the subject is more technical, perhaps a gathering more like this Council is appropriate, with the skills, gifts and talents of members coming to the fore *irrespective* of whether they are bishops, clergy or laity. Or on another occasion there may be some more juridical question to decide, where the Primate of each Church is more appropriate, he—or she—who in the end has to exercise authority in each particular Church.

All that I propose does not suggest we can avoid confusion or solve problems neatly. No matter how externally authoritative synods or councils may appear to be, they have sometimes erred. No matter how representative a body may be, its decisions may be mistaken. In the end, the whole Church has to receive the decisions of popes, bishops, councils and synods. And this can never be reduced to a legal process. In acceptance or rejection, in modification or development, the whole people of God have an essential and decisive part to play. Here is the ultimate assurance of truth in the Church: the gift of the Holy Spirit in baptism to the whole Body of Christ.

So there must always be something provisional about a Church that sees its life as pilgrimage, as a Church which is always learning. It can get things wrong. 'Only the hand that erases can write the true thing,' wrote Meister Eckhart.

God is not hemmed in by our successes, nor is he caught out by our failures. We shall never learn from our mistakes unless we are prepared to make some. This sense of venturing ourselves for Christ should give us a confidence that is denied to those who think that we can build some man-made perfect order of peace and justice. The lesson of history is that if men leave out God they become less than human. If they deny eternity, they cannot find contentment in time. If they will have none of the heavenly city, they cannot build a tolerable society on earth.

Of course we must fight for peace and justice. Of course we must take the lead in the stewardship of our precious planet Earth. But in the end it is Christ who will bring in the Kingdom and not ourselves. I am happy to believe that in the Anglican Communion we have the least unsatisfactory way of leading a world Church.

During my archiepiscopate I have tried to be a representative focus for our unity, not for the sake of some monolithic international structure, but for the sake of the rich diversity I spoke of at the beginning of this address.

To believe that there is some perfect system of church government is to succumb to a fantasy, to a dream which hinders the hearing of the Gospel. Dietrich Bonhoeffer had some harsh words for those who want to impose their visionary dreams upon the Church. They are words we do well to heed, for they also lead us to the heart of what it is to be the Church.

> He who loves his dream of a community more than the Christian community itself becomes a destroyer of the latter, even though his personal intentions may be ever so honest and earnest and sacrificial.
>
> God hates visionary dreaming; it makes the dreamer proud and pretentious. God has already laid the only foundation of our fellowship because He has bound us together in one body with other Christians in Jesus Christ . . . we thank God for what he has done for us. We thank God for giving us brethren who live by his call, by his forgiveness, and by his promise. When the morning mists of dreams vanish, then dawns the bright day of Christian fellowship.

I pray that we may know the bright day of Christian fellowship.

CHAIRMAN'S ADDRESS

By the Venerable Yong Ping Chung, Bishop-elect of Sabah, on Sunday 22 July 1990 in Cardiff City Council Chamber at the opening of the eighth meeting of the Anglican Consultative Council.

Taking the risk of being repetitive and saying the obvious, may I first and foremost take this opportunity to express publicly our gratitude and thanksgiving by praising and giving honour to God for gathering us all together in Wales for this eighth meeting of the Anglican Consultative Council.

It is very right and proper that our first official act together as a family was to join our Welsh brothers and sisters, our hosts, in the celebration of the Eucharist at the great Llandaff Cathedral. I was told that our public witness of praise and thanksgiving as a family was televised throughout the British Isles. May God, through the miracle of this modern technology, use this public worship for his own glory.

As each one of us puts aside two weeks of our busy routine, and travels many miles away from our own Church, our own land and our own work, I am sure we are aware that we are not at all alone. We are supported by prayers from every corner of the earth. Archbishop French Chang-Him, a former ACC member, and the Bishop of Dhaka, Bangladesh, have sent us a telex and letter to wish us every blessing in our meeting. President George Bush has also sent us a message. Among other things President Bush said, 'My special greetings to your president, Archbishop Runcie, on the occasion of his last meeting of the Council before his retirement ... As you meet to chart a course for the future of the Anglican Communion you are also helping to renew the spirit of brotherhood and charity that unites its members. I commend you for your dedicated efforts, and I know that millions of people join me in praying for the success of your discussions.'

These are the expressions of goodwill, support and prayers for, as well as high expectations of, our meeting in the next two weeks. It is indeed encouraging and gratifying to be assured of such solid support. It is of course also very frightening that there is such a high expectation of our two weeks together.

I am very clear in my mind that if our work is only for our selfish ends in order to win our own agenda, we do not deserve such support; if our work is done by our own human effort we can never be able to fulfil such high expectation. Thus we dare not move on our own and do things for our own selfish ends. Each morning we will gather all we have and all we are at the altar of God, and offer all to God so that he can use the humble offering of ourselves for the good of his Church and his world. Each evening we will again gather in prayers to praise and thank him for what he is achieving through the guidance of his Holy Spirit. It is appropriate to use the words of Micah 6.8:

> And what does the Lord ask of you: only this, to act justly,
>
> to love tenderly and to walk humbly with your God.

As far as Micah was concerned, acting justly and loving tenderly is part and parcel of walking humbly with God. To him, unless a person has experienced a personal encounter with the living God, unless a life is touched and transformed by the Spirit of God, unless a person humbly submits and is committed to God, that witness, that work and that life cannot be an authentic reflection of the life of God. Our daily Eucharist and daily prayers at the Council are a symbol of this humble walk with God. This must be the source of life, power and authority in our daily work. Our discussions on 'Spirituality and justice', 'Mission, culture and human development', 'Evangelism and communication' or 'Unity and creation' will be authentically of God if, and only if, we put into them what is *from* God.

I regard myself as very privileged to have eleven years of close association with the Anglican Consultative Council. May I put this in picture form? I stepped into the family ship called MV ACC that set sail from London, Ontario, Canada, 8-18 May 1979. I remember that I was in fear and trembling as I arrived at ACC-4, because I had never been in such high-powered circles before in my life. As a simple young priest from a small Church called Diocese of Sabah, I was curious, and feeling strange about everything that was going on at my first ACC meeting. Secretly I admired people like the then Archbishop of Canterbury, Archbishop Coggan, the Chairlady, the late Dr Marion Kelleran, the Secretary General, Bishop John Howe, and many other outstanding and articulate leaders from different parts of the world. They seemed to know what they were doing; they were able to express clearly and convincingly what they believed. I must confess that, without looking at the ACC-4 report, I could not remember what we discussed in ACC-4. To be honest, I did not really understand everything discussed and all the procedures and proceedings of that meeting. But ACC-4 left a deep, deep impression on me. What touched me most was not the resolutions, even though we passed quite a lot of resolutions and some of them were no doubt very important, nor the vast subjects that were discussed—believe it or not, even in those days we also had four Sections to deal with a wide range of

36

topics—but I was touched by the family life, the sharing, the mutual support, the love and the burdens carried for each other in the Anglican family of God. I remember vividly the day the delegates from Uganda arrived at Huron College, after the devastating experience of Idi Amin; the tremendous story they shared with us of the courage and suffering of the people of God in Uganda; the wonderful celebration we had with them. I was moved and touched and felt proud to belong to such a family. Nothing can ever replace this quality of shared life based on the bond of the love of Jesus Christ.

So I returned to Sabah after ACC-4 and continued my calling and work as a simple parish priest. I was very much encouraged and strengthened by that common life in Christ I had shared for ten days with my brothers and sisters in Christ. At every appropriate opportunity I share with my people and colleagues what it means to belong to such a world-wide family. I hope and pray that similar kinds of personal experience will also enrich each one of us in this ACC-8 meeting, so that we will have more than just resolutions, reports and budget to take back to our own Church.

Each subsequent ACC meeting then became a high point in my life and spiritual journey. I looked forward to each meeting with eagerness and expectation. So I continued to sail with MV ACC, to Newcastle, England, 8-18 September 1981, and to Badagry, Nigeria, 17-27 July 1984. With the passage of time and the call at each port the bonds of affection grew stronger and deeper in me. My election to be the fourth Chairman of ACC in Badagry, Nigeria, came as a great surprise and shock to me. Even today I am still trembling from the shock of that election. In my more sober moments I often said to myself, 'Oh stupid Ping Chung, how dare you even accept the nomination and election to be Chairman of this world-wide body called the Anglican Consultative Council!' With a deep sense of awe, privilege, fear and trembling I must say I have enjoyed my term as Chairman of ACC very much. Therefore I love this family, and this family is built on love. My chairmanship years saw MV ACC travel from Nigeria to Singapore (1987), then the Lambeth Conference of 1988 and now Wales in 1990. I will be getting off the ship after this meeting of ACC. It is only right that I use this opportunity to express my deep gratitude to the many people who have helped me to enjoy my years as Chairman of this Council. I want to give thanks to God for bringing the following colleagues, friends, brothers and sisters in Christ into my life during my years of association with ACC. I want to thank each and every one of them from the bottom of my heart.

First, I thank the Archbishop of Canterbury, my metropolitan and my respected friend and brother in Christ. Of course, we all realise how much he has done for ACC and the Anglican Communion. There will be occasions when this can be expressed formally. But in this personal reflection I recall the time in Nigeria, just before the chairmanship election, I went to him for counsel, because he was my metropolitan. I was hoping that he would discourage me from accepting the nomination. But he strongly encouraged me to accept, at the same time very lovingly and pastorally reminding me that being nominated also opened up the possibility of being disappointed when not elected. I hope I am not embarassing him by being so personal. Throughout my years as Chairman, Archbishop Runcie has always been so encouraging, supportive, caring and loving to me and my family. May I say thank you to you, Archbishop?

Secondly, I thank our Vice-Chairman, Canon Colin Craston, and my colleagues in the Standing Committee. I am sure many times they must have been weary of my strange, unorthodox and unsystematic Chinese way of conducting the business of the ACC Standing Committee. I admire their endurance, I appreciate their dedication, and I can assure you we all share common traits of sensitivity, care, love and concern as we deal with the business of this Council as a Standing Committee. In every discussion, in every decision there is always at the top of our minds the pastoral effect on those who are involved. I want to thank them all for teaching me so much.

Thirdly, I thank our Secretary General and his staff. I don't think anyone in this chamber and around our Communion will ever doubt the efficiency and effectiveness of our Secretary General, Canon Samuel Van Culin, and his staff. But more important than this efficiency and effectiveness, I find that the Secretary General and the staff share with us a common vision, the vision of holding, strengthening, deepening and enlarging the family of the Anglican Communion—together. Very often they go beyond the call of duty and serve us ever so well. This staff is now serving the three visible instruments of unity in our family, namely the Lambeth Conference, the Primates' Meeting and the ACC. You will see the expression of this in the letterhead and stationery we are about to use. As our expression of confidence in love, your far-sighted Standing Committee has invited Canon Van Culin to extend his term of being Secretary General for a further two years after his present term ends, to the end of 1994, so that he can help us through to ACC-9 and a little beyond. I want to thank Sam Van Culin and the staff for their support and their contribution to this life of our family.

Fourthly, I thank each one of our members and participants past and present. At each ACC meeting about one-third of our members retire. Yet I am always thankful that the quality of life, work and witness brought by our members and participants at each ACC meeting is always so real and authentic. I praise God for the privilege of touching base with all of you. I thank you for bringing yourselves, your life in Christ and your Church to this family gathering. Thank you for sharing all these so generously.

On reflecting about the theme of the family, I discern a very basic character in the ACC family. This is very akin to the concept of family I know well as a Chinese. In the Chinese mind the family is most important. That is why my name is Yong Ping Chung: Yong, surname/family name first; personal name Ping Chung second. Each family shares everything and pulls together. We talk about how well we can give and share in the family. We never demand our own rights and privileges in the family. All members of the family are expected to share, to support and to uphold the family with what they have. I treasure the equal representation of our membership in ACC. This enables the big Church, small Church, wealthy Church and not-so-wealthy Church to consult together and to contribute together in building up this family. I value the inclusion of the three orders of our Church in this ACC meeting. This gives bishops, clergy and lay people a share in taking our joint responsibility in the family's affairs seriously.

I am grateful that our right of membership does not depend upon the amount of money we can pay into the family coffers. I praise God for those wealthier brothers and sisters of this family who continue to put their resources into the support and upholding of the family. Confronted by budget cuts in our own Church, it is so easy to succumb to the pressure of cutting our support of this family budget. Of course, there is always some small number of individual members of the family who try to get out of making their contribution into the family budget, even if they are able to. The final analysis, I believe, depends upon our vision, our commitment to the future of the family. It is my hope and prayer that this ACC meeting will, through its worship together, sharing together and working together, strengthen this family of ours.

In my simple, Chinese way I will say that we belong to this family at the point of our conversion, or when we are born again, or when we encounter the living God personally, or when we commit our life to Jesus Christ (or however you like to put it). No transformation of life is possible until and unless our life is touched by the life of God. I have no quarrel with the insistence of Christians who express concern for

The Venerable Yong Ping Chung, Bishop-elect of Sabah and Chairman of ACC-8, speaking in Cardiff City Council Chamber.

the wider and larger issues: culture, justice, human development, unity and creation and so on and so forth! I don't even worry if we want to define evangelism in a bigger and wider context, as long we do not leave out the cornerstone of a new life in Jesus Christ. The Decade of Evangelism can easily slip out of our fingers if we talk about every important issue and topic under the sun, and even bring all sorts of sophisticated methods to bear, but neglect to present to the people around us the claim of Christ in the life of each individual. We need to share with the world our authentic life in Christ. We need to present to the world the challenge that in Christ there is life, and life more abundantly. I give thanks to God that all over our Communion we have many, many family members who have this experience of the life of Christ. As they experience this new life, they are eager to share the life with others. They are the most powerful evangelists we have as a Communion. They are the front-line missionaries in our Church. In our deliberations, let us not forget these brothers and sisters in Christ. Let us ground and root our work and life together so that we can help these brothers and sisters in Christ to identify the same vision with us, to feel that they are being encouraged, valued and supported. There are millions of people praying for us with great expectations that we will guide and lead the Anglican Communion into the Decade of Evangelism for the transformation of life to the glory of God. They expect to hear God speaking through us to them and to the world.

As I look back over my eleven years with the ACC, I count myself greatly privileged. I give thanks to my God for what he has given me. MV ACC has travelled a long way since my first day going on board the ship. Today, on the point of getting off the ship, I want to share with you a vision and a hope. This comes from the assurance of Jesus to Nathanael in John 1.50:

> You believe that just because I said: I saw you under the fig tree. You will see greater things than that.

Jesus said to Nathanael: Nathanael, don't worry. I saw you under the fig tree, just a common, simple but genuine human being. I will take you as you are and make you something great. You will see and do greater things than what you will ever think possible.

Jesus is saying to us today: Don't worry. I see you in your Church, full of human errors and human faults, a very ordinary organisation; but you have brought it to me. I will sanctify it. I promise you that I will use it, and you will see greater things than that.

Indeed, the Lord is not finished with ACC yet; he wants to mould it and use it for greater things. You shall see greater things than that.

SECRETARY GENERAL'S REVIEW

By the Reverend Canon Samuel Van Culin on Sunday 22 July 1990 in Cardiff City Council Chamber at the opening of the eighth meeting of the Anglican Consultative Council.

Meeting as we are in this great chamber of public discourse and debate belonging to the City Council of Cardiff, I am reminded of the story of a member of parliament in another chamber in Westminster in London. In preparing for a major address to parliament he fell into a nasty argument with his speech writer on the evening they were preparing a major speech for his delivery the next morning in the House of Commons. In a fury the member of parliament stormed out of his office at midnight, shouting to his speech writer: 'Now finish that speech so that I can have it at 10 a.m. tomorrow morning . . . and then you are fired.'

The next morning he dashed through his office, picked up the speech that was waiting for him, and ran into the House of Commons in time to be recognised and deliver it. He was well into his speech, at page 9, and moving to his concluding arguments, saying, 'And now, Mr Speaker, I challenge this House to think seriously about . . . ', when he turned the page and found written in a bold hand across page 10: 'From here on, you are on your own.'

This meeting is 'page 10' for me and the ACC. At this meeting we will say goodbye to our President of nine years, Archbishop Runcie, and to our Chairman, Yong Ping Chung, who has been a member for 11 years. They have provided the framework for me as Secretary General since my appointment, and with their departure it is true to say 'we will be on our own'.

This is not the point for farewells, which we will share at the conclusion of our meetings, but it is right that we should start our proceedings by recognising our great debt to them for the enormous gifts they have given to this Council in time, loving support, stimulation, guidance and dedication.

For these two gracious people, who are indeed gifts of God, we praise his holy name.

At this first meeting of the Council following the Lambeth Conference 1988, your work must include both reflection on what the Conference achieved and also planning for the future. The experience of these past five years suggests, I believe, that this Council carries a major responsibility in shaping the agenda for the next Lambeth Conference. That work begins now and will be continued at the following meetings of the Council which have already been tentatively projected. The schedule of inter-Anglican meetings for this decade, approved by the Primates and your Standing Committee last year in Cyprus, demonstrates a commitment to work together more closely. They have set out a plan for meetings of Primates and the ACC prior to the next Lambeth Conference in 1998, and our work together will proceed within that framework and with the next Archbishop of Canterbury.

In the area of evangelism and mission the Lambeth Conference called on each Province and Diocese of the Anglican Communion, in co-operation with other Christians, to make the closing years of this millennium a 'Decade of Evangelism'. Of all the actions and resolutions of the Lambeth Conference, none has caught the imagination and commitment of the Church as universally and effectively as this one has. The Primates at their meeting in Cyprus last year brought their hopes for the Decade of Evangelism into focus in a concise statement which they issued to the Churches. This has provided a comprehensive framework within which all of the Churches are at present reflecting and planning, and each is acting in its own particular way in response to the call to a Decade of Evangelism.

Since the meeting of the Primates we have been able to welcome an Adviser on the Decade of Evangelism to the ACC staff in London, in the person of the Revd Canon Robert Renouf, who has been seconded until June 1991 by the Episcopal Church USA, which is covering his complete salary and benefits. He has been of enormous assistance to us in our initial efforts to implement the Lambeth Conference resolution, and we hope to integrate the responsibilities that he presently carries into a newly designed job description for the post of Mission, Social Issues and Evangelism Officer on our staff. Recommendations related to this proposed post will come before you in the report from the Inter-Anglican Finance Committee.

At this meeting of the Council you will deal directly with the long-term implications of the Decade of Evangelism in the Section on Evangelism and Communication, chaired by Mrs Pamela Chinnis. She has said of her Section's work that 'unlike previous ACC meetings that were preparations for Lambeth, we now have before us the opportunity for "moving on", strengthening our commitment to better communications and effective evangelism'. We are fortunate to have the Right Revd Roger Herft, Bishop of the Diocese of Waikato in the Church of the Province of New Zealand, who will address the Council on the subject of 'The Gospel and communication', and serve us as a consultant on this subject. He will demonstrate, I am confident, how deeply the content of evangelism and the forms of communication are related to each other.

Our ability to communicate in the Communion today is much more advanced and mature than it was five years ago. The Inter-Anglican Publishing Network, our increasing capacity to utilise audio-visual materials and video productions, and the emerging Inter-Anglican Information Network (IAIN) are striking examples of this development. So is our improved capacity in publishing. Although we have a long way to go in perfecting our publishing programme, it is worth noting that each individual publishing account is in credit. In religious publishing terms that can be considered an achievement! We are particularly indebted to three publishing houses: The Anglican Book Centre, Toronto, and its Director and Publisher the Revd Michael

Lloyd; Church House Publishing, London, and its Publishing Manager Robin Brookes; and Forward Movement Publications, USA, and its Director and Editor the Revd Dr Charles Long. I estimate that the various contributions made by the three amount to at least a full-time staff person's time at the ACC Secretariat. I want them to realise how much their contribution is appreciated throughout the Anglican Communion. While on the subject of publishing, I want to welcome and thank Mr Roger Coleman, who will act as Editor of the Report of this Council meeting. A former Publishing Director for Cambridge University Press, he recently acted as co-ordinating secretary, under the chairmanship of Lord Coggan, to the Joint Committee of the Churches on The Revised English Bible, a version we will use during the ACC-8 meeting. It is an encouragement to note that advance orders for the Report of this meeting to date total 3,100.

The Inter-Anglican Information Network, popularly known as IAIN, was the subject of a resolution at the Lambeth Conference, which asked the ACC to explore the establishment of a telecommunications network linked to every Province, and urged the creation of a telecommunications centre for the Communion on the model we are developing with IAIN. We are now taking the first steps to develop the capacity to set this telecommunications network in place, as a result of a generous grant and a long-term commitment to the challenge by Trinity Church, Wall Street, in New York, for which we are deeply grateful. As a result we now have a full-time Director of the IAIN project on our staff in the person of the Revd Fred Howard, formerly Director of Mission Information Services for the Episcopal Church in the United States. You have his report before you, which will I hope encourage you (as it does me) to have confidence that we can enter this complex world of technology with professional competence and understanding, and provide a service of growing importance for the Churches of the Anglican Communion and the wider ecumenical community.

In addition to publishing and telecommunications developments we have been able to take some steps in developing the use of video-cassette technology in the last five years. This was especially evident in our preparations for the Lambeth Conference, when we were able to produce *Lambeth '88: The Call*. You will have detected that our initiatives in communication are made possible through funding completely outside our core budget. This is not less true in the production of visual aids and videos, since we have depended on the services of the Revd Robert Browne for undertaking the responsibility of both their financing and their production. He is currently working on the compilation of a video on the Decade of Evangelism for distribution and use throughout the Communion.

Unity was the great theme of the Lambeth Conference 1988. The Conference itself made its commitment to the unity of the Church unmistakably clear. This was demonstrated in resolutions about Anglican reports on dialogues with Lutheran, Oriental Orthodox, Orthodox, Reformed and Roman Catholic Churches. Many observers have described the Lambeth Conference 1988 as an ecumenical watershed for the Anglican Communion. The Primates at their meeting in Cyprus in April 1989 endorsed the establishment of a regular Inter-Anglican Ecumenical Advisory Group, and you have in your hands for this meeting the initial report of their work together. Taking their lead from the address of the Archbishop of Canterbury, 'The nature of the unity we seek', and recognising the urgent importance of including concern for the environment in all our considerations of unity and mission, your Standing Committee has organised a special Section on Unity and Creation at this meeting of the Council under the chairmanship of Mr Edgar Bradley. He has already observed that 'to the extent that the Primates have an overriding concern for the unity of the Church in the face of diversity, I expect the ACC to concentrate on celebrating variety in the Church'. He refers to the message of creation as 'unity of variety' and goes on to say that development of this concept may well be the main emphasis of the Section.

Further reinforcing this, we recall that in his opening address the Archbishop of Canterbury gave the Lambeth Conference and the wider Church a theological vision, of enormous breadth and profound thoughtfulness, on the relationship between the unity of the Church, the unity of humanity, and the unity of creation. 'It is within this broad agenda—God's agenda for the unity of all creation,' he said, 'that we must set the no less divine agenda of Christian unity and the unity of the Anglican Communion.'

We have made a commitment to the search for the unity of humanity in the appointment of the Right Revd Sir Paul Reeves, presently Governor General of New Zealand, as the representative of the ACC and the Archbishop of Canterbury to the United Nations. He will be accredited to the Economic and Social Council and will begin his work in New York City in early 1991. We are grateful to the Presiding Bishop of the Episcopal Church USA, the Bishop of New York, General Theological Seminary, and the Rector and Grants Committee of Trinity Church, Wall Street, in New York City, for providing the support system and location for this important initiative. Sir Paul will link our Communion with the important work of the UN world-wide!

The work of the section on Mission and Ministry at the Lambeth Conference ranged effectively and thoughtfully over a wide variety of the most important challenges and concerns for our Communion. Not only did the resolution on the Decade of Evangelism come from this section, but also resolutions on the ministry of the laity, the training of bishops, and important reflections and suggestions about the renewal of the Church in liturgy. The Mission Issues and Strategy Advisory Group (MISAG), whose terms of reference were approved by this Council in Singapore, has built on these insights of the Lambeth Conference in preparing its interim report. The members of MISAG represent a wide cross-section of missionary societies and agencies, mission theologians, provincial missionary planners, and ecumenical mission colleagues. Their work in the interim report reflects the various mission challenges we face right across the life of the Anglican Communion.

The third International Anglican Liturgical Consultation, which met in York, England, in August 1989, built its work on reflections from the Lambeth Conference on the renewal of the Church in liturgy, concentrating on the two specific resolutions of the Conference related to this subject: Resolutions 22 on 'Christ and Culture' and 47 on 'Liturgical Freedom'. The theme of its conference was 'Down to Earth Worship: Liturgical Inculturation and the Anglican Communion'. You have its report for consideration. The Primates, in Cyprus, asked the International Anglican Liturgical Consultation to carry responsibility for the concerns for liturgy which the ACC meeting in Singapore had hoped could be incorporated into the responsibilities of a new Inter-Anglican Liturgical Commission. It has proved to be financially impossible to inaugurate such a commission. We are grateful to the Anglican Liturgical Consultation for taking on this responsibility, and for the effective way in which Colin James, the Bishop of Winchester and a member of this Council, has undertaken the special responsibility of liaison with the Liturgical Consultation on behalf both of the Primates' Meeting and of this Council. Since the adoption of this proposal by the Primates we have been able to add to our staff a Co-ordinator for the Anglican Liturgical Network in the person of the Revd Paul Gibson who has been seconded, part-time, by the Anglican Church of Canada. That Church supports his salary and benefits. He is our staff liaison with the Anglican Liturgical Consultation and, in co-operation with Bishop James, is building up and co-ordinating the development of an important and more effective liturgical network in the Churches of the Communion.

In January 1988 the first International Conference of Young Anglicans took place in Belfast. We are indebted to the Church of Ireland for all that it did to welcome over 200 young Anglicans from around the world and support their work so effectively. The themes of the conference were the same as those of the Lambeth Conference, and the two youth co-opted members of the ACC, together with two youth consultants, were able to contribute effectively to the Lambeth Conference. In the light of the success of the first Young Anglicans Conference a second one is being planned to take place in 1993 in Canada. The first meeting of the Planning Group for that Conference will take place in Scotland next week, and our ACC Youth Members will be in contact with that Planning Group so as to be able to report to the Council during this meeting about plans for Canada 1993.

These activities reflect initiatives to implement the work of the Lambeth Conference on mission and ministry, and were taken into account when your Standing Committee decided that a special Section of this meeting of the Council should meet under the heading of Mission, Culture and Human Development, with Archbishop George Browne as chairperson. He has already said of the work of his Section that 'we are entering a second stage of activity, and ACC-8 can help us see more clearly the way ahead'. Unfortunately Archbishop Browne is not able to be at this meeting because he is so deeply involved in the search for a resolution of the tragic events taking place at this time in Liberia. We are grateful to the Very Revd Walter Asbil, Bishop Coadjutor elect of the Diocese of Niagara in Canada, for accepting the responsibility to chair this Section.

The Section on Spirituality and Justice, to be chaired by Canon Winston Ndungane, is an effort to draw together work that was done in the section on Christianity and the Social Order as well as the section on Doctrinal and Pastoral Concerns at the Lambeth Conference. The Section will explore the way in which this Council can help the Church understand both the spiritual and social dimensions of its ministry to those suffering from AIDS, to voiceless minorities, and to Churches and Christian communities dealing with the consequences of injustice and violence. While we do not have reports at this meeting from the Peace and Justice Network, the Refugee and Migration Network and the Family Network, we do have up-to-date information about the growing AIDS crisis. We also have a wealth of experience from our own members about the powerful and cruel injustices that continue to assert themselves and affect human communities and our Churches throughout the world. Canon Ndungane has spoken of his hope that through his Section this meeting of the ACC can find a way to assist with 'a coming into being of a Church that has been led by true prayer to see itself as a remnant called by God to witness to the crucified and risen Lord in a world that needs to experience once more the Christian meaning of death and life'.

When we think seriously about the place of the Anglican Consultative Council and its responsibilities within the total life of the Anglican Communion in these years immediately following the Lambeth Conference of 1988, we must focus on the related concerns of identity and authority. Your Standing Committee has already taken an important initiative in this regard, and in consultation with the Primates' Meeting in Cyprus, 1989, it has prepared the statement 'The Anglican Communion: Identity and authority'. In his address to this Council our President, the Archbishop of Canterbury, has given us a thoughtful and imaginative reflection on the subject of identity and authority for the Anglican Communion, which will be an important resource to the Council as it discusses this subject. In addition, the Standing Committee has set a framework for your discussion by providing specific questions addressed to each of the Sections, so that the results of your deliberations can be collated and integrated.

We have asked the Churches of the Communion to send us reflections on this document 'The Anglican Communion: Identity and authority'. These responses are available to assist you in the discussion of this important subject.

Because of the nature of the subject of authority and identity, our discussions are liable to remain too abstract and theoretical. To avoid this danger I have felt it necessary to focus our attention on some practical possibilities. I have requested the preparation of a special paper on 'Provincial constitutions: Autonomy and interdependence', which has been produced by the Revd David Chaplin. He has provided us with a study of the constitutional implications of the theological work we have been doing together in a variety of ways over the past few years on Anglican identity and authority. I am aware that this paper touches on sensitive issues within the life of the Churches of our Communion, but such issues cannot be avoided if we are to take seriously the question of identity and authority. It is a paper that I hope gives us the opportunity to focus our minds on what we do and do not consider right and advisable. The paper reminds us that in a Communion of Churches such as ours, our provincial constitutions must inevitably reflect our ecclesiology: our structures must be designed to provide a unitive framework for our diversity. I hope this

Council meeting can offer the Churches specific comment and advice on this matter.

We are pleased to have with us the Revd Professor Jaci Maraschin, a priest of the Igreja Episcopal do Brasil and Professor of Theology at the Ecumenical Post-Graduate Programme on Science of Religion in São Paulo. He will address the Council on the nature of our Communion and help us to think through some of the implications of identity, authority and communion.

I conclude these remarks as I began them, with a personal tribute. Canon Martin Mbwana served this Council and the Churches of the Communion as Secretary for Mission and Social Concerns. Martin's death earlier this year has left all of us with a deep sense of loss mixed with gratitude for his gifts, to us who worked so closely with him and to the development of the Anglican Communion.

Martin was part of the leadership of a new and young Church in Tanzania. This autonomous and self-governing Church was a divided Church, because of its development out of various missionary societies representing the variety and diversity which is in Anglicanism. SPG, UMCA, BCMS, CMS and many other missionary societies had all poured their resources of people and money and prayer into the building up of parts of the Church of Tanzania. Martin was himself the proud heir to part of that creativity, the so-called high-church and Catholic part. His heroes would always be the brave and devout fathers of the Universities Mission to Central Africa and the Society for the Propagation of the Gospel, now joined together in the USPG. But his world required a wider vision of the whole Church.

As he started at St Mark's Theological College and continued through the years as Secretary of the Province of Tanzania, this wider vision for the whole Church of Tanzania, a new and more mature communion of Churches, emerged and grew in Martin. His work was the expression of this. As the second Provincial Secretary he served Archbishop Sepeku, Archbishop Kahurunanga and Archbishop Ramadhani. He was part of the growing pains of a new provincial structure, of a new liturgy, of a new prayer book, of a new national responsibility, of a new ecumenical initiative with all the churches in Tanzania. They were years of outreach into new congregations, new dioceses, new evangelistic initiatives, new struggles to find the proper role of the Church in the building of the nation. They were the years of Julius Nyerere. These were Martin's years.

Those of us who worked with Martin in those exciting years came to appreciate and respect his deep and creative pastoral gifts, his sharp observations, his balanced judgement, and his resilient spirit occasionally resulting in stubborn insistence. He had to be stubborn in those days. He helped us with these qualities to build and develop the Anglican Communion. We need to remind ourselves that we cannot build a healthy local Church in isolation from the Church Universal, and we cannot develop a world-wide communion of Churches apart from the vision and resources of the local Church. The world-wide Church cannot exist unless it is local. The new heaven and the new earth unfold together.

Martin Mbwana was one of the new breed of people who helped to unfold this new Church. He moved as easily and creatively in the Church in Papua New Guinea, in Australia, in Scotland, in the West Indies, as he did in the Church in Dodoma and Arusha in Tanga and in Dar es Salaam. This is because he had a vision and experience of the Church as one and whole.

Martin lived that vision for many of us. We thank God for him and for that vision.

As we prepare to enter a new millennium in a world that has come to recognise afresh the need to wonder at God's creation, and to cherish and preserve God's gifts of unity, let us embrace and work for a new earth within the vision of a new heaven.

Special Papers

GROWING IN COMMUNION

Jaci Maraschin
Priest of the Igreja Episcopal do Brasil
Professor of Theology,
Post-Graduate Programme on Science of Education, São Paulo

Let me start by telling you about a recurring experience in my ministry. Being in charge of a sort of base community in São Paulo, chiefly interested in the development of spiritual life and, consequently, in good liturgy and Brazilian liturgical music, we have been growing in theological understanding of the Gospel and, therefore, of the mission of the Church in our contemporary society. We are not so much interested as perhaps my bishop would like in keeping statistics. When my friends from other churches meet me, they ask the inevitable questions: How was the service? Did you have many people there? My answer is: I did not count the number of people in the congregation. I know, however, that we all enjoyed the liturgy and I am sure we are growing in communion.

Growing in numbers?

I know that the Church, in order to fulfil its work in the world, has to grow. We have been told that the Church has to grow. It is like the law of the market place in our capitalist societies. We do not even pause to think about it. The present Decade of Evangelism may mean to many precisely this: growing in numbers of members. We all know how to make our money grow through bank accounts with interest. So, we dream of congregations with interest. What parish priest does not use the parable of the talents in this way? We all know the slogan: each member of the Church brings another prospective member. This is part of our culture. It is the spirit of growing.

The Christian doctrine of creation sees the world as a growing reality—growing in the measurable sense. Seeds, stars, flowers, fruits, animals and everything else were created by God as growing realities. As human beings we also received the vocation to grow, to grow and to

51

multiply ourselves. It seems that multiplication was intended to be a vital sign of life. Abraham received the challenge from God to multiply enormously in order to be the father of many nations (Gen. 17.2,4). Jesus was also interested in numbers. He sent his disciples into the world to preach the Gospel and to make disciples from all nations. Discipleship was simply taken as increasing the number of disciples.

Growing in this sense was considered a sign of life and the result of a blessing. It seems to be a law in nature and in society. According to the Scriptures, however, growth is never for its own sake. It never becomes an obsession. Growing has a rhythm and an aim. A tree grows according to its nature. It grows to the measure of its own capability. Growth follows the terms of God's laws. But we can certainly interfere in the rhythm of nature and accelerate or decrease it. Things, animals and people can grow normally or abnormally. Technology is trying to accelerate the growing of fruits, vegetables and animals for the sake of profit. We try to introduce in the very being of things that which in the end violates reality. Instead of transformation and real growth, we create deformities. In the light of this universal law of growing, the Church sees herself as a growing part of reality.

Like everybody else, I want to see people in the churches, in the concert halls, in the parks and in the streets all around. I like to see this ACC assembly full of people. But I do not believe that growing in numbers, in this quantitative way, is the real purpose of evangelism or of mission. There must be something deeper to motivate our work in the Church and in the world. Growing in numbers could be, perhaps, the result of our mission, but not the foundation of it.

Living in Latin America, I am witnessing an astonishing growth of Pentecostal sects, African religions, occultism and some eastern forms of spirituality. Compared with them, our traditional Churches are not growing. Some of us are puzzled. Some of us are even obsessed by what I would call a 'statistical neurosis', looking constantly for reasons and causes for the phenomenon. On the other hand, there are also some of us asking what is the real relation of numerical growth to the effectiveness of the Gospel today.

Any Church may at different moments of history show signs of growing or of decay. During the days of the earthly ministry of Jesus, while we cannot speak in a true sense about the Church as we know it today, growth in the numbers of followers was not a remarkable sign of the time. Jesus even finished his earthly ministry on the cross surrounded by very few disciples. He was deserted by some of his closest friends. On the other hand, as the result of Jesus's resurrection and of the coming of the Holy Spirit, we read in the book of Acts of the extraordinary growth of the Church. The interpreters of that time thought that the growth was the result of the work of the Spirit. So most of us believe.

As I have already pointed out, the traditional or 'mainstream' Churches are not growing today. They fail to grow on account of different causes and circumstances. In the meeting of Partners in Mission held this year in Brazil, and in the related celebration of the centennial of the Igreja Episcopal do Brasil, the question of growth was part of the agenda. In a meeting with the Presiding Bishop of the Episcopal Church in the USA, Edmond Browning, in Porto Alegre, after his announcement of a new era of partnership between the Church he was representing and ours in Brazil, a young priest asked him if it should not be taken into consideration by the American church that the Brazilian Church was not growing sufficiently in numbers. Should not the American partners analyse the causes?

The young priest had in the back of his mind a suspicion that when a Church does not grow, there must be something wrong in that Church. Bishop Browning, if I remember his words, said from his experience in America that the chief emphasis of the Church should not rest in numerical growth but in the proclamation of the gospel of liberation, which means to be faithful to God, doing his mission in the world. We know that many people have left the American Church because of its deep involvement with the struggle of the poor and the persecuted, and because it denounces injustice and has opened its mind to listen with courage and faith, in prayer, to what the Holy Spirit is teaching it. For that reason the American Church has accepted the ordination of women and is pursuing liturgical reform.

But for the Brazilian priest the situation was a very different one. A Church may fail to grow because she is affected by a sort of disease that kills her energies and entangles her life. The difference between the witness of the American Church and the difficulties of the Brazilian priest was this: in the first case the Church has lost some people because of her love for truth and justice; in the second case the Church is not attracting new people to join in her mission because she is alien to the social, cultural and political life of the country.

Growth in communion

The question at stake is not numerical growth, as important as that may be. Growing in numbers is a sociological phenomenon that can be studied and detected by scientific means. It does not testify to the truth. We Anglicans are interested in growing in communion. This is a current topic of discourse in our Churches, but not all of us understand the same thing by it.

FAITH AND ORDER

Growing in communion, in the first place, may mean something institutional. As a member of the Commission of Faith and Order of the World Council of Churches (WCC) for many years, I like to relate the question of communion to questions of faith and order. The Commission of Faith and Order is supposed to be the theological commission of the WCC assigned to give deep foundations to the work to be done. It seems to me, looking at what we have been doing through so many years, that we have given too much attention to order and very small attention to faith. Sometimes I think that the Church is divided not because of faith but because of order. If this is true, we would say that what binds us together is certainly 'faith' (we all say that 'we believe'), but in our practical experience and history it is 'order' that threatens that unity. Unhappily, we cannot have faith without order, although we may have order without faith.

In the Anglican Communion I feel a very strange move towards 'order' that frightens me. Each time we meet, we try to see some institutional elements which would, in the long run, be the infallible means of communion. After all, we call ourselves 'the Anglican Communion' and we want to justify why it is a communion and not just a federation of Churches or Provinces. Is communion a merely rhetorical term?

As precarious and humble institutional beings we always look for institutions. We say that we are a communion because we are Churches bound together through different levels of authority and decision-making bodies. Then, we look into ourselves. Growing in communion means, in this context, the development of a denominational awareness, a sense of belonging in the sociological sense.

It is very common today to speak of four institutions devoted to 'communion' in our Anglican family of Churches: the Archbishop of Canterbury, the Lambeth Conferences, the Primates' Meetings, and our own ACC. The four institutions were born out of historical needs and respond in some degree to the development of our denominational consciousness and denominational identification. However, denominational consciousness and denominational identification are not equivalent to communion.

One of the reports of ACC had the expressive title *Bonds of*

Affection. This is the most we are able to say about the four institutions just mentioned: they are bonds of affection. The most long-standing of these bonds is, of course, the Archbishop of Canterbury. His position as a *primus inter pares* has been accepted throughout the world as a sign of apostolicity and continuity. Indeed, it was around his leadership that a communion of Churches came into existence after so many centuries.

We in Latin America understand history, and we know that the Latin American Church cannot have as its head a Latin American Jesus, born perhaps in Nicaragua, or twelve apostles coming from ancient Aztec or Aymara cultures. As much as we would like to have the See of Canterbury in Mexico City or in Brasilia, we understand that this is impossible. We cannot change history or tradition. We are happy with God's design, and believe that a symbol like this can help us to be in a Church that has decided to belong to the whole of the catholic Church and not to remain for ever as a sect.

As much as we all love the Archbishop of Canterbury, however, he cannot be the source of our communion. We are not in communion because we have the Archbishop of Canterbury, but we have the Archbishop of Canterbury because we are in communion with him and with each other. Behind and above the Archbishop of Canterbury there exists another power holding us together in communion. The Archbishop is one of the many signs and symbols of that communion.

The other institutions are not as easy to acknowledge as the Archbishop of Canterbury. If, for example, we accept the doctrine that says 'where the bishop is, there is the Church', then Lambeth would be the real focus of unity and of communion at the institutional level amongst us. But increasingly our theology not only denies the Cyprian affirmation, but puts in its place a concept which comes from the Bible and is very alive, especially in third world countries. It says that the Church is 'the people of God', of which bishops are only a part, important as they may be, but still a part. I do not deny the importance of a meeting of bishops coming from all over the world. But I have serious doubts that the Lambeth Conference could have the same status as the Archbishop of Canterbury at a symbolic level. To me as a non-English Anglican, the accent on the Englishness of Lambeth challenges the intention of catholicity in our Communion. As far as fidelity to history is concerned, the symbol of the Archbishop of Canterbury should be a sufficient institution working for communion. Some of us in the third world countries which are not linked historically to the British Empire see Lambeth as a remnant of colonial times. Some of us are tempted to compare the gathering of bishops at Lambeth to colonies coming to court to get the blessing of the imperial monarch.

At the institutional level, the Primates' Meeting has been mentioned frequently as another occasion for improving communion amongst Anglicans. I think this is the weakest of all the organs of our Church. Primates do not have the same status in all national or regional Provinces. In some of them, as in the Brazilian Church for example, he is the president of the Synod and can be changed every two years by the vote of the Synod. In some other Provinces primates have canonical power equivalent to an archbishop. Some of them even hold the title of archbishop. I have no problem with the meeting of all our primates around the world. I think they face difficult situations and they need mutual counselling. But I cannot see how that kind of meeting could be a means to real communion. Indeed, the three levels of institutional symbols of communion so far mentioned represent a pyramidal view of a hierarchical Church. There on top is the Archbishop of Canterbury. Then, around him, the primates, followed by the bishops of the Church all around the world.

This hierarchical image contrasts vividly with the image of a Church of the people, growing from the grass roots, expanded through base communities, and holding faithfully the principle of the priesthood of all believers. Some will argue that this is an 'episcopal' Church. Yes, indeed, but there is no good reason why an episcopal Church should degenerate into mere 'episcopalism'. It was precisely this that the first Anglican Congress in Latin America, in Panama, challenged when the group studying the episcopate asked for more democratic participation of all members of the Church in church affairs.

The last institution at this level is the Anglican Consultative Council. And this is the only real, all-embracing and fully democratic body in the Anglican Communion, somehow involving in itself the three former institutions and providing a forum remarkable for its representativeness and for the frequency of its meetings. It is much more like the heart of the Church Visible.

The order of importance we give to these institutions does not matter. They belong to our tradition, and the fact of being open to criticism only witnesses to their transitory and historical condition. They are the outcome of communion instead of being the agents of communion.

THEOLOGY

Growing in communion may mean something theological. Those of us, like myself, who are suspicious of institutions (not because of their existence, but because of the temptations of institutionalism) would perhaps welcome another level of searching for communion, the theological level. This level is best expressed in the much praised and quoted Lambeth–Chicago Quadrilateral. We Anglicans have produced this short and clear document, and through this manifesto we have told the world on what grounds we may have communion within ourselves and with any other Christian body. As you all know, the principles are: the Bible, the creeds, the two sacraments of the Gospel, and the apostolic ministry. Is it a sufficient guideline for growing in communion? When we say 'the Bible', we affirm it to be 'the rule and ultimate standard of faith'. Of course no Christian Church would depart from this principle. But it is precisely in the interpretation of the Bible that Churches and Christians lost their unity and communion.

What is the meaning today of 'rule and standard of faith', after so much divergent research and conclusions from biblical scholars around the world? Already in 1965, in a memorable conference between theologians of the Church of England and the German Evangelical Church, Dr Martin Schmidt reminded us that 'the concept of Scripture becomes flexible. It is understood,' he said, 'neither as a dogmatic arsenal of inerrant and absolutely valid statements all on the same level, nor as the infallible product of an untouchable sacred history. Rather, it enters within the lowliness of all history, within concrete historicity with all its uncertainties, its "chances", and its dependence on subjective accounts and prejudices. Scripture is history in its full sense.'[1]

In other words, he was saying that it is impossible to think of the Bible without hermeneutics, and hermeneutic shows us today innumerable conflicts related to tradition, culture and ideology. In Latin America, for instance, many Christians experience communion and grow in communion, with what we call 'the popular reading of the Bible'. A new dimension of understanding of the Christian life, and a new spirituality, spring from the poor, the oppressed and the illiterate. Yet I was challenged by first world biblical scholars when defending this 'popular reading of the Bible'. What is important to observe is that the Lambeth–Chicago Quadrilateral statement on the Bible is not able to produce communion, nor is it able to lead us into growing in communion. People grow in communion when, led by the Spirit of God, they read the Bible in their own context and relate that reading to their own human experience, and especially when they relate it to the struggle for liberation in their own situation.

When we turn to the creeds we have another kind of problem. The Quadrilateral states that the Nicene Creed is a 'sufficient statement of the Christian faith'. Here again we are in the realm of order. If we pay attention to linguistics today and try to understand the limits of human discourse, what would 'sufficient statement' mean? 'Sufficient' for whom? No statement of the Christian faith can be, by its very nature, 'sufficient'. If we could interpret 'sufficient' as 'provisional', yes, that would do. In this case 'falsifiability' is better than 'sufficiency', as Karl Popper would say with reference to scientific law.

It is not because we are able to recite the creeds together that we are in communion. We hope that Christians will confess the faith together, in communion. What is at stake in the confession of the Christian faith is not the formula, but the togetherness of the confession. I challenged and still challenge the work we are doing in the Faith and Order Commission trying to explain the apostolic faith through the study of the Nicene Creed. The question of the togetherness of the confession is what is really important. How can the oppressors confess the same faith together with the oppressed? What is the meaning of communion in situations like that? Are we trying to say that a simple recitation of a formula is a sufficient means for growing in communion? But we have been confessing the same creed in the liturgies of many divided Churches. We do it; the Orthodox Church does it; the Roman Catholic Church repeats the same creed, and also some Protestant Churches. If the creeds or the Nicene Creed are 'sufficient' statements of our faith, why do we state that same faith and still insist on our sinful disunity?

We cannot grow in communion only through the recital of the creeds. We need something more deep and more powerful. Turning to the two sacraments of the Gospel, the Quadrilateral says that they express for all 'the corporate life of the whole fellowship in and with Christ'. It is probable that we could say that in relation to Baptism, though still some Christian denominations practise a second baptism. But can we say the same about the Eucharist? The Lord's Table has been stolen by Churches and denominations, and instead of being the Lord's Table it has become the Table of the Orthodox, the Roman Catholics or even the Anglicans in some sections of our own Communion. Can we baptize for disunity or celebrate the sacrament of Holy Communion for disunity?

Finally, we have the question of the ministry. This means a 'ministry acknowledged by every part of the Church as possessing the inward call of the Spirit but also the commission of Christ and the authority of the whole body'. Though the Quadrilateral does not speak of 'apostolic succession' it seems that, in general, that has been the current interpretation of 'ministry' at this point. Since 1920 until now there has been a tendency to interpret 'apostolic ministry' as 'apostolic succession'. It is, however, a mistake to think of apostolic succession as only a mechanical act with some magic element in it. The World Council of Churches' *Baptism, eucharist and ministry* document says that 'In churches which practise the succession through the episcopate, it is increasingly recognized that a continuity in apostolic faith, worship and mission has been preserved in churches which have not retained the form of historic episcopate. This recognition finds additional support in the fact that the reality and function of the episcopal ministry have been preserved in many of these churches, with or without the title "bishop".'[2] I do not think it would be fair to go back to the sterile controversies about the 'validity' of orders in the different Churches. Orders are valid because they belong to the inner life of the Church: the Church is not the Church because the orders are valid.

What is communion?

Communion is *koinonia. Koinonia* is not something that we can build. We can grow in *koinonia.* If we turn to the teaching of the New Testament we soon detect two senses of the verb *koinonein*: communion enjoyed and therefore perceptible by all, and communion expressed through different acts. Many passages of the New Testament demonstrate the origin of communion in the being and action of the Holy Spirit. It is always a gift of the Spirit. It is immersed also in the being and activity of the Holy Trinity: 'The grace of the Lord Jesus Christ, and the love of God, and the fellowship of the Holy Spirit, be with you all' (2 Cor 13.14). In this salutation, the source of the announced gifts are the persons of the Holy Trinity: Jesus Christ gives grace (because he is grace); God the Father gives love (because he is love); and the Holy Spirit gives communion (because he is communion). As we are able to say that growing in grace means following Jesus, and growing in love is to worship God, so we should also say that growing in communion is living with the Spirit the new life that he brings to all. The new life of the Holy Spirit is dynamic and free. This is the same life announced by Jesus in his preaching, ministry, death and resurrection, threatening the old life of sin and disunity.

For that reason we cannot just maintain our old disrupted structures and add the new life of the Spirit. The result would be artificial. The new life of the Spirit is dangerous to the institutional life of the Church and of nations. It judges them and calls them to repentance and amendment of life.

Theology today has to learn from the social sciences some guidelines for understanding its own task. I think that much of the trouble with the development of 'communion' in the Churches comes from the absence of sociological analysis in what we do and say. Let us start, for example, with the concept of 'ideology'. As so many scholars have said, ideology has the principal function of avoiding public recognition of the foundations of power. The norms and structures we have are not put up for discussion (they are said to be non-negotiable), because they are presented as final and true. The power is legitimated through a discourse which avoids criticism. According to this perspective, canon law is to be obeyed, not discussed. According to the ideological vision, communion is something to be created by instruments which may be technical or structural. It cannot be free and depends on the exercise of human power. At the bureaucratic level of society all decisions affecting the majority of citizens are considered technical problems to be decided by experts. At the bureaucratic level of church affairs the same may happen, and when we give to experts the task of deciding for the whole body, we are accepting the bureaucratic ideal of our technological society, instead of being led by the inspiration and by the power of the Holy Spirit which acts in and through the whole body.

Communion is also communication. The current theories of communication recognise as a fundamental element of analysis of reality the presence of noise in the process of interchange of messages. This means that no discourse reaches its goal completely. It is also obstructed by noise. Noise is that which disrupts not only communication but also communion. Noise is the opposite of silence and music. In the Kingdom of God we are promised to be released from noise, in order to get silence and music as gifts of eternal life.

The theological question posed to us in the face of our contradictions is as follows: how can we grow in communion in the midst of a world of noise and disruption? This is a very difficult question. We have already seen how easy it is to turn the question of growth into the question of numbers. This is very similar to the technological axiom of our present capitalist society: if it works it is good. The technological society never poses the question of truth. From the side of capitalism, if things give profit they are necessarily good. So, growing in numbers and in profit becomes the aim of the non-critical mind. But also we have criticised the position which starts from institutions and organisations in order to analyse growing and communion. We have seen that our institutions and organisations are not able to create communion. If we attain communion through the gift of the Spirit, then institutions may have a place in the life of the Church and a relevant role to play.

My intention is to emphasise the relativity of institutions. The Kingdom of God is not an institution. Then I have tried to show that we cannot grow in communion through mere theological debate. Theological debate and reflection are results of communion, but they do not produce communion. The only source of communion is the Holy Spirit, the giver of life. In the light of the Spirit we see how communion is related to life and how it has to be seen as the chief aim of the mission in our days, and always.

But communion is not an idea. The disruption of communion is related to the disruption of communication. We have this perennial message, which we call 'Gospel', rendered in linguistic terms. The German professor Jürgen Habermas has made a relevant contribution to the discussion of this question in our time. Though he speaks from the principles of critical theory and orients his prophetic words to the world at large, I think we could profit from them, in order to face the difficult question of growing in communion. In brief, he affirms that our communication is distorted because we do not experience a 'linguistic ideal situation', in which the communication would not be distorted by external contingent effects, nor by coercion coming from the communication structure itself.[3] This would be possible if all interested people could participate in the game of language, with equal opportunities of argumentation, interpretation and recommendation. This means, also, a new kind of society where people would not be led by coercion but by love. It excludes, of course, all sorts of neurosis and false consciousness. According to Habermas, this would result in a model of communicative action of the most pure quality. This model is utopian. It presupposes a social order which does not exist at this moment. Nevertheless, this order can be anticipated, and it is precisely the possibility of that anticipation which makes criticism possible and creative.

Trying to apply this principle to the realm of theology or, more precisely, to the life of the Christian Church, we see some similarity to the definition of the 'Protestant principle' in the theology of Paul Tillich. The 'Protestant principle' is the possibility inherent in the Gospel to refuse all kinds of idolatry which are so easily inserted into the life of the Church. When we are able to exercise this critical principle in the analysis of our institutions and programmes, we may be entering the way leading us into communion. In other words, we cannot grow in communion if we do not develop among ourselves the prophetic principle of self-criticism and of dependence on the work of the Holy Spirit.

Communion is also related to truth. And truth is not a proposition, not a doctrinal statement, nor a creed. Truth is a person, precisely the one who said: 'I am the way, the truth and the life.' So, as Habermas would say, we have a theoretical discourse, which is theology in the traditional way, and a practical discourse, which is life. There is always a distance between these two discourses. But there must be a relation between them.

It is the same relation found between *logos* and being. This relation is always a struggle. *Logos* or reason wants to express being, but being is much more than what *logos* could apprehend. The final stage of communion is the attainment of a life in truth and love. 'God is love', we have all heard from our first experience in the life of the Church. But the love of God is nothing if it is not reflected in our society and our Church. Returning to some of our earlier statements, I would say that because love is the possibility of overcoming noise in our processes of communication, it is also the first condition for communion. We believe that God so loved the world that he gave his Son to the end that all who believe in him may have eternal life. Because of God's love he gave his Son. He did not give us 'his book' or 'his theology', nor even 'his Church'. This gift of the Son, which is the revelation of his love, became the necessary truth for us. And the Spirit is the power opening our eyes and minds to understand this, not as a council declaration nor as a theological formula, but as a way of life.

The call for growth in communion heard at the convocation of this meeting is equally a call to revise and to criticise ways which may seem to be well established and beyond any doubt. We are called to grow in communion through our own institutions: but the way to grow in communion through these institutions means an effort to relativise them, exorcising them, so to speak, from the devils of authoritarianism, of absolutism and of idolatry. We are called to grow in communion through our theological work. Our theological work, to be the servant of this growth, has to allow people full participation in the debate and to start a process leading to what in some places of the third world is already called a 'theology by the people'.

Growing together

We cannot expect to grow in communion looking to the top of our pyramidal hierarchical organisation. Frederick Denison Maurice, the nineteenth-century Anglican theologian, said that theology was 'digging'. We have to come down from the top to the base in order to dig. And we cannot 'dig' alone. In Brazil we sing throughout the country that God is calling us 'to a new life'. We sing that the 'time is ripe for changing, the moment is now'. Then, everybody in the congregation, hand in hand, makes a big circle, and dancing they sing: 'It is God who calls us to work together for justice. Let us walk together: no-one can go alone.'[4] We can grow in communion when we come down from our higher positions, from our sublime institutions, and join the people in this digging together, which is the building of communion. It means going to the depth of our faith.

Let me finish this paper with an illustration from my country. The Archbishop of Canterbury, visiting São Paulo, was received by the Roman Catholic Cardinal, Dom Paulo Evaristo Arns, in his cathedral. This ecumenical celebration of the centennial of the Brazilian Episcopal Church represented to my understanding the most significant liturgical action there. We had representatives of many Christian bodies, like the Orthodox, the Lutherans, the Presbyterians, the Methodists, besides the Roman Catholics and, of course, the Anglicans.

The ceremony was typically Brazilian. Too noisy, perhaps, to the British ears of our Archbishop. But full of the same Spirit wishing to lead us in communion. The Archbishop was saluted by the Cardinal as a messenger of peace and union. And we, from all the different Churches, saluted each other with the Peace. But the most significant symbolic action was when the Cardinal and the Archbishop came down from the high altar to the nave of the large church, full of people of all sorts and conditions, but chiefly from the poorer sections of our society. They did not ask what was the meaning of 'Anglicanism' in order to salute the Most Reverend Robert Runcie. They did not speak English. But these thousands of poor people received him as someone coming from God, and it was moving to see the crowd trying to touch his cope, to kiss his hand and to have his blessing.

This is a good symbol for what I have been trying to say all the time in this paper. The Church has to come down to the people. Communion will grow only if it means communion with the people and among the people, and if it transcends all the walls of separation built in history by our narrowness and lack of vision. 'So', as the song goes, 'come and join! Get in a circle with all the people . . . let us walk together: no-one can go alone!'

REFERENCES

1   R.R. Williams (ed.), *Authority and the church* (SPCK, 1965), p 21
2   W. Lazareth, *Growing together in baptism, eucharist and ministry* (Geneva, 1982), p 104
3   J. Habermas, 'Vorbereitende Bemerkungen zu einer Theorie der kommunikativen Competenz' in: J. Habermas u. N. Luhman, *Theorie der Gesellschaft oder Sozial-technologie*, p 137
4   J. Maraschin, *Brazilian songs of worship* (Geneva, 1989) p 55

THE GOSPEL AND COMMUNICATION

Roger Herft
Bishop of the Diocese of Waikato
Church of the Province of New Zealand

Gras fyddo i chwi, a thangnefedd
Grace be with you and peace
yu enw ein Harglwydd Iesu Grist.
in the name of our Lord Jesus Christ.
Cyfarchion cynnes i chwi oddiwith Aotearoa New Zealand!
Greetings warm to you from Aotearoa New Zealand!
Diolch o galon am eich croeso
Thank you from the heart for your welcome
a'ch cyfeillgarwch cynnes.
and your friendship warm.
Bendith Duw a fyddo gyda ni oll!
The blessing of God be with us all!

Thank you for your invitation to be present and to address this meeting. It is an honour and privilege for me to be among such a representative gathering. Some have suggested that the reason for my being chosen is my accent. It is supposed to have a slight Welsh lilt. It's good to be here in beautiful Wales.

I stand here not alone, for I am linked with several people from the past and present who have shaped and continue to shape my life. I acknowledge some common links in this body: Bishop Lakshman Wickremesinghe, the one who placed the grace of confirmation on me, and whose life, friendship and example has had a profound effect on my journey; the Bishop of Kurunagala, Andrew Kumarage, here present, who was my teacher and spiritual guide; Archbishop Paul Reeves, that great disturber of comfortable 'Church zones'. In addition there are the women of Aotearoa, New Zealand, who continue to challenge and change my patriarchal concepts of theology and church structure; the elders of my own heritage and the ones from the Maori world who have taught me an 'angry patience'; women, men and children—my family, wife and two boys included—who have disturbed, enhanced and enabled me to try and be real about following the Christ of Galilee.

Coming into Wales on the coach a few days ago, my eye caught two stickers placed above the driver's head:

DON'T PUT YOUR MOUTH INTO MOTION BEFORE YOUR BRAIN'S IN GEAR	I MAY NOT BE SMART, GOOD LOOKING, OR RICH, BUT I AM AVAILABLE

Listening and *Open Availability:* two of the basic communication tools for evangelism!

The Gospel and communication

A Sunday school teacher had taken the class through the crucifixion of Jesus Christ in graphic detail. She then sent the children away to paint a picture of the event. She was somewhat surprised by one child's depiction of the drama. Calvary Hill, the three crosses, ferocious looking soldiers were all in place; but hovering over the crosses in the midst of the dark clouds was a plane with the pilot looking down precariously at the scene below. Perturbed by this drawing, the teacher called the child and enquired about this strange phenomenon. Swiftly came the reply: 'You told us that Jesus suffered under Pontius Pilate; that's Pontius the Pilot.'

Communicating the Gospel can be risky, for you never know if the message that is received is the one you sent.

There is also the story told of the professor of theology who wished to enter into the spirit of the Decade of Evangelism. Going up to a group of young people gathered around a cassette-player where they were swinging away, he cried out, 'Your gathering is an ecclesial paradigm of the great eschatological reality of God's eternal kingdom. It is an existential expression of a fiduciary search, which the very ground of our being has responded to in the logos. Do any of you feel convicted to offer your substance to this ontological reality.' There was a stony silence; then one replied, 'Choice, Man! Got a smoke?' Communication, even when received with affirmative sounds, may not have actually communicated.

Words can mean very different things. A great deal depends not on the one who speaks, but on the one who interprets the message upon hearing it.

I am conscious that as I place before you some views on the Gospel and communication, we face some risks in the giving and in the receiving. There are obviously some limitations in how I communicate. My place of birth, my upbringing, the social structure of the societies that have formed me, and the context of my past and present work, naturally form the basis upon which I speak and act.

I was brought up and lived most of my life in Sri Lanka; consequently the living faiths of the world are ones which I have had ready contact with: Buddhism, Hinduism, Islam, Christianity and Marxism are living realities, for I went to school with them! The issues of poverty, major racial conflicts and the tension of religious and political ideologies are part of who I am. They have questioned my faith and shaped my thinking.

The history of Christianity, its arrival with the Portuguese, Dutch and British, influenced the way that Gospel was communicated and responded to in Sri Lanka. Sadhu Sudar Singh questioned the imported nature of Christianity in India when he said, 'Christianity is a potted plant and people have begun to worship the pot rather than the plant.' The need for Jesus Christ to be seen as Saviour of the peoples of Sri Lanka, and not as a colonial legacy, was a constant challenge for me. Indigenous cultures and faiths had to be taken seriously. Communication as listening prior to teaching or proclaiming has always been a part of my understanding and expression of evangelism.

I was invited to New Zealand by the Methodist Church, which had debated long and hard about seeking a world-famous evangelist to speak at large rallies in the four major cities. They decided not to go for the evangelist, but instead invited an Anglican priest from Asia who could speak reasonable English to go into 15 parish centres to help people discover their Gospel stories and how they could best share them in the local community.

A recent survey of the religious factors in New Zealand society concluded that in its European sector, New Zealand is one of the most secular countries in the world. Communicating the Gospel in a culture that is 'anti-faith', and at various levels is prejudiced against matters spiritual, brings its own limitations.

I have learnt, by living in New Zealand, that while the stark material poverty of the East is not as evident, there is a deep poverty of belonging and identity. The desire to acknowledge the indigenous people, the working out of the partnership between women and men, children and adults, young and old, the loss of community, the passion for sport, shopping and the self-cult indicate some of the factors that form both my communication and response today.

Some of my conviction and learning about evangelism and communication is what I want to share with you now.

Life is communication

Life is about communication. Every one of us uses a wide variety of ways to let others know how we feel, what we think and why we do things in a particular way.

It is now suggested by some medical experts that communication begins from the time a foetus is a few weeks old. Communication is the art of letting your presence be felt in the universe. Some are obviously more adept at this than others.

In the Christian understanding of life, communication is vital because the Creator of all communicates. An essential function of God is revelation. The Bible tells us that God is a God who communicates. The Genesis stories of creation are about God's communication—of setting nature free for its true destiny, the destiny of communicating with the one who created all. The words used in the creation narratives are full of communication symbols. God creates, speaks, sees, touches, shapes, walks, questions. The serpent is seen as one who confuses or casts doubt on God's communication.

The Bishop-elect of Sabah has a good story about the serpent. He told me once that the problem in the Garden of Eden was that Adam and Eve were Europeans. That's why they were fascinated by the apple. If they had been Chinese, he said, they would have ignored the apple and eaten the snake! Even food communicates.

In the Exodus we see God communicating as Saviour, as one who redeems. The prophetic voice in the Bible is a strong communication from God. Events in history, visions, dreams, natural disasters, the life and times of political leaders were all interpreted in order to recognise what God was saying at any given time, and how best the chosen people could respond. Even catastrophic events that seemed to reflect an absence of God's communication, such as the Exile, are seen as ways in which God enables people to get an idea of the divine character. The communication is both to individuals and to the community, and the purpose of the communication is for a better understanding and the building up of a closer relationship.

In the fullness of time God communicates in a unique way through a person, Jesus of Nazareth. As the Gospel of John so aptly puts it, 'The Word became flesh and dwelt among us, and we have seen the glory of God.' The very nature of God, that communicated itself at creation in setting all things free to communicate with God, now takes on the mantle of creation—a communication within time and space, and in a form that cannot be ignored. Jesus used the communication methods of his day: stories and parables, humour and question, paradox and sign all assisted in arresting attention and obtaining a response.

The New Testament writers are at pains to tell us that the Christ event is no chance or accidental happening. God's central act of communication is well planned. Those familiar with the study of the inter-testament period know this for a fact. It takes the context of the time seriously: the flowering of Greek language and culture, the roads and seas open for travel, the justice of Rome that tried to curb the wayward spirit, the decadence and poverty of the mystery religions. It recognises the need to have a core group for in-depth planning, and sets out within given limits to proclaim the news. It reaches out to meet people's needs and acknowledges the cost of risky communication.

The life, ministry, death and resurrection communicate the very essence of God as one whose life-waves reach out beyond words to action. The New Testament uses the special word 'grace'—God's love in the act of Christ—to describe this amazing art of risky communication.

Communicating the good news of God in Jesus Christ is the central activity of those who come into contact with the Living Word.

The Acts of the Apostles describes the way in which the community of the Church communicated the good news of Jesus Christ in their world. The activity of evangelism is seen primarily as God's task, and they allow themselves to be the vessels of communication. Communication took every form and shape then known to the world: word of mouth, witnessing to the power of God to change life, healing, signs, miracles, martyrdom, worship, example, the life of the community, writing, preaching, nurture, caring, a willingness to stand up to government and to those in high places, a passion for right living at both the individual and the social level.

The shift in focus from Jerusalem to Rome displayed in the Acts of the Apostles is a description of God's living story staking a claim in the market places of the then known world. The Gospel faces competition from other thought forms, it incurs anger from enterprising business folk (remember the silversmiths at Ephesus!) and has to face up to the criticism of how best to continue its journey to other market places when some of the chief communicators are stifled by being cast into prison or are silenced by death.

The writing of the New Testament, the life and witness of the Church throughout its history are responses to the demand to proclaim.

What of our times?

Communication in global culture

Communication today has been revolutionised; the silicon chip has altered the way we talk to each other. Screens, terminals, and the cult of instant access to information have changed the way we live. The concept of the global village has become real with modern forms of transport and telecommunication. TV has brought the world into our living rooms. We are informed of events around the world as they happen. The technological advancement in the last twenty years has created a new electronic culture that seeks to control the desires and responses of people in the remotest parts of the earth. It is ironic that in an age in which freedom of choice has become a major catchword, the skill and manipulative techniques of high-tech marketing and advertising have an unhealthy control over so many lives. Whatever political, economic or sociological forces are behind all the news, programmes and products that are placed before us, we cannot escape this all-pervasive culture.

This global culture, in which we seek to communicate the Gospel, has affected almost every nation on earth, directly or indirectly. Some of its main features are:

(a) It is strongly individualistic: the central question on any matter is, 'What's in it for me? How does it profit me?'

(b) It is sensate: feeling, touching, seeing, hearing, smelling, tasting are the basis upon which value is placed in respect of any product. If it feels good it must be okay.

(c) The gratification must be instant. It does not wait till tomorrow to feel the 'kick'. If something does not provide an instant, 'now' reaction, then its value diminishes. The faster the product arrives, the more pleasing it is. A cynic has remarked that the status of a city depends on how many fast-food outlets it provides for its inhabitants.

(d) Things and experiences are not made to last. It is a throw-away generation. A five-year life cycle is considered to be a long time. The Anglican Church is ancient in the light of this. The impact on culture, language and relationships has been most significant.

(e) It is pluralistic. It acknowledges a wide variety of value systems. Religion and religious experiences from the West and East are offered in a sort of smorgasbord or buffet; picking, choosing and consuming to fit individual ideas is the name of the game.

(f) Leisure, sport and recreation seek to create an identity for a community that is a set of isolated individuals who do not believe they need each other to live out the intricate patterns of life. Religion with its highly fragmented denominations is seen as one among many optional leisure activities. It is not considered compulsory for living.

(g) The essence of what we live by needs to be scientifically tested. Mystery becomes synonymous with ignorance and superstition. Science and technology take on the qualities of prayer and pleading, and the minds of white-coated technicians become the gods to be acknowledged. Trust them; they know what to do! One of the major consequences of the scientific and rational world view is its 'anti' attitude to tradition, ritual and religion. Because of its strong emphasis on the 'now', things from even the recent past are considered relics that have no functional value. With no positive ritual or tradition to be identified with, the human psyche seeks compensation in negative ritual and bizarre customs. If Hollywood has its finger on the pulse of the way most people think and feel, its focus on the occult and mystery, horror and sanctified violence, show that negative ritual has good box-office value.

This is the context of global culture. The global or universal culture is a culture of the young. It is relayed in their music and language. Communication takes place in this world for those below the age of 40 through what has been called the AVP principle: auditory, visual and participatory.

An extreme example of using high technology is the way Rod Stewart, the 'hot rocker', describes how he communicates with his children: 'Thanks to modern technology, we keep in touch with each other through fax machines. I send faxes to their schools which their teachers go and read out for them. You know, it's better than just a phone call. They love it.'

Many of our youth have grown up in a learning environment which is different from that of a large majority in the Church. They are inductive in their approach to learning and do not easily enter into the deductive style of teaching and preaching still so prevalent in our Churches. Our music, our worship patterns, our fellowship need not fall into the trap of being gimmicky or faddish, but they will certainly have to move from the passive type referred to by a bishop walking through a fish stall, who, seeing row upon row of glassy cod eyes glaring lifelessly at him, was heard to remark, 'Those frozen eyes: how they remind me of the congregation I see from my pulpit every Sunday!'

It is recognised that within this global culture there are several movements that are more local or national which challenge the assumptions of development made by technology and scientific advancement. These small but powerful groups seek to question the values fostered by the global culture. Questions surrounding the environment, alternative health care, the liberation movements that refuse to acknowledge the oppression of ideologies of right or left, the re-awakening of ancient religions, the rise of spirit life-force communities, the Green movement, the increasing demand for a change from patriarchy, the move towards more fundamentalist attitudes within the major religious faiths, are all examples of these responses and challenges.

Anglicans and communication

How do we communicate the Gospel in this complex milieu?

By and large, Anglicans have had a 'Private and confidential' label over their faith life. Like sex and politics it has been kept for the bedroom. If there is one commandment of Christ that Anglicans have kept with some degree of joy, it is Jesus's admonition to the three disciples after the Transfiguration, 'See that you tell no one.' The messianic secret is one we have guarded closely.

We have claimed that we are a Church for the people. Our pastoral ministries are open to all. We will do to anyone what they want done—be it baptism, marriage, confirmation, burials—without seeking any commitment from those who require our services.

The essence of our character is that of 'being' rather than 'doing': a holy presence, not a loud promotion. There is a dignity about us. It is said that even if we die as a Communion, we shall see to it that it is done with dignity and due liturgical order!

By and large we tend to be somewhat aristocratic. Everyone knows who we are; they can come to us if they wish! We do not want to be tarnished with the spills and thrills, the bargaining and prodding of the market place, so our non-communication has paid dividends. The people in the market place of the world make other choices or no choice at all.

Even those who claim nominal allegiance we treat with silent respect. We are therefore termed the organisation with the largest number of sleeping partners. How would we have to change if we wanted a gear shift from maintenance to mission? How do we respond to the market place in the Decade of Evangelism? Lofty ideals and good intentions are not going to communicate. Neither is our long-standing good name. Even the Jaguars, Rovers and Rolls Royces must get into the market place these days!

The four-fold definition of mission, which ACC-6 was responsible for, has taken root in several of our Provinces and parishes. We now know on paper what mission is. There has always been a great danger in Western tradition in believing that, once something has been defined and written, the question has been answered and the problem solved. The four-fold formula of Proclaiming, Nurturing, Caring, and Transforming now needs to be used in the market place.

Communicating in the market place

The New Testament was born and communicated in the market place. It vied and jostled for a place in the hearts and minds of people who were offered a wide variety of choices. Evangelism will take place if we take the market place seriously.

In a book entitled *Sell like a pro,* Sherrill Estes makes some interesting points about selling: 'Selling is the thread that holds society together. No matter what a person does for a living, his or her job is related in some way to selling.'

'Selling is nothing more than making others believe in what you believe in, or value what you value.'

'To function in a selling society, a person or product must make a claim and live up to it.'

In a new sales technique called consultive selling, she suggests four basic requirements for making others believe in what you have to offer:

Product knowledge: the salesperson and the company must have an in-depth knowledge of the product. They must be convinced of the benefits of the product for themselves; otherwise it won't sell.

Selling skills must seek to use the unique character of each salesperson. The days of salesperson stereotypes are gone.

Attitude must be positive and must seek to develop long-term trusting relationships. It is said that 68 per cent of those who change from one company to another do so on account of the attitude of the business representatives.

Selling demands sellers *who set goals that are realistic,* challenging and worthwhile. If you aim nowhere, you are likely to hit it! If you have no goals, then you will meander on with no purpose or intention!

I am not sure that God was into consultive selling, but the four basic requirements suggested are certainly followed in God's communication. The Bible speaks about 'knowledge' of God as the basis for life. The New Testament portrays those who proclaimed Jesus as Lord as speaking out of an in-depth knowledge of Christ, and aware of the benefits of knowing and loving the one who revealed God in such a unique way. They were sure of the quality of their product and knew its benefits.

The Scriptures are full of 'unique' salespersons for God, some of them strong and bold, clever and popular; others are foolish, weak, cowardly and even eccentric. Yet each is used to portray the truth of God in their lives. The choice of the twelve disciples is a good example of miscellaneous uniqueness!

The God story in the Bible and in the history of the world is a story of long-term trust and of faithfulness. The message of the Bible, of Christ and the Church, is of a God who does not give up on us.

The nature and character of God is of one who carefully plans and orders the universe. In the midst of chaos God's Spirit enables cosmos. Jesus set goals that were realistic, challenging and worthwhile. 'The Spirit of the Lord is upon me, for he has anointed me to bring good news to the poor, sight to the blind, to set free the prisoners from their chains, to proclaim the acceptable year of the Lord.' The great commission from Jesus to the disciples is to set them goals. 'Go therefore into all the world and preach the Gospel. You shall be my witnesses in Judea, in Samaria and to the uttermost parts of the world.' The Gospel writers had goals. They took context, language and style seriously. They had a specific aim in writing. The movement of the Church in the Acts of the Apostles shows a Church willing to move in a direction, Jerusalem to Rome being stage one.

Origen, one of the early Christian writers, refers to those who made it their goal to share Christ; Christians do all in their power to spread the word of faith all over the world. Some of them make it the business of their life to wander not only from city to city, but from town to town and village to village, to win converts for the Lord.

A major gear shift if we are to seek to communicate is that we must believe in this need to proclaim and be intentional about it in our life and ministry. D.T. Niles, the scholar and teacher from Sri Lanka, said it simply: 'Evangelism is following Christ. Only those who have felt the grip of Christ will realise what evangelism involves; to be

THE EVANGELIST
EVERY CHURCH SHOULD HAVE ONE

A gold finger for pointing to heaven

Eyes that can look through people

Nose capable of sniffing out sin anywhere

A loud voice in order to drown out everybody else

An irresistible smile with an on-off switch

A bighead is usual

White hair giving the head-in-the-clouds effect

Ears with an inclination to deafness

A large tongue for speaking the language of angels

A non-crushable suit for ease of travel anywhere in the world.

Bible with a push-button pop-up latest version device

Knees with an anti-knocking regulator

Large feet for stepping on the opposition.

This caricature is meant for fun yet in some respects it illustrates the picture we sometimes have of an evangelist.

Reproduced by permission from the CPAS course 'Come back Evangelism—all is forgiven!' by Gordon Jones.

74

evangelised means not merely to change a label or a community, but such a cleansing of the spirit and a change of direction in the soul, that in one more life God's purpose for all is achieved, and through one more life God's will on earth is done.'

A Decade of Evangelism will get nowhere without us having a personal knowledge and conviction that Christ is Lord, and being willing to share it with passionate zeal, not on a haphazard basis but with the care and preparation that God uses in getting through to us. At the heart of it all is the call to 'fish'; here is a challenging modern parable from John Drescher:

A PARABLE OF FISHLESS FISHERMEN

Now it came to pass that a group existed who called themselves fishermen. Week after week, month after month, and year after year those who called themselves fishermen met in meetings and talked about their call to fish. Year after year, they carefully defined what fishing means, defended fishing as an occupation, declared that fishing is always to be a primary task of fishermen; in fact, that there should be a Decade of Fishing!

Continually they searched for new and better methods of fishing. Further, they said, 'The fishing industry exists by fishing as fire exists by burning'. They loved slogans such as 'Fishing is the task of every fisherman', and 'Every fisherman is a fisher'. They sponsored costly nation-wide and world-wide congresses to discuss fishing and to promote fishing, and hear about all the ways of fishing, such as the new fishing equipment, fish calls, and whether any new bait had been discovered.

Many who felt the call to be fishermen responded. They were commissioned and sent to fish. They engaged in all kinds of occupations. They built power plants to pump water for fish and tractors to excavate new waterways. Some also said that they wanted to be part of the fishing party, but they felt called to furnish fishing equipment. Others felt their job was to relate to the fish in a good way so the fish would know the difference between good and bad fishermen. Others felt that simply letting the fish know they were nice, land-loving neighbours and how loving and kind they were was more than enough. After one stirring meeting on 'The Necessity of Fishing', one young fellow left the meeting and went fishing. The next day he reported he had caught two outstanding fish. He was honoured for his excellent catch and scheduled to visit all the big meetings possible to tell how he did it. So he quit his fishing in order to have time to tell about the experience to the other fishermen.

Now it's true that many of the fishermen sacrificed and put up with all kinds of difficulties.

Imagine how hurt some were when one day a person suggested that those who don't catch fish were really not fishermen, no matter how much they claimed to be. Yet it did sound correct. Are people fishermen if year after year they never catch a fish?

The questions then before us are: How do we fish in the hi-tech waters of our world? How do we attract the fish whose lives are filled with the food of concern and suffering, or who are satisfied and content with the surplus of what they have?

The Isaiah Agenda

The call to fish—the demand to fish—requires us to be aware of the waters and the fish. It does not require us to be callous with people or to be exclusive. To catch fish, you must know where the fish are!

Raymond Fung from the WCC speaks about this strategy in relation to what he calls the Isaiah Agenda (Isaiah 65.20-23). Here, the preferred society is one in which 'children do not die, old people live full lives, those who build houses live in them and those who plant the vineyards eat the fruit': the whole community where each lives for all and all live for each. Fung challenges us to be partners with those who seek this common good no matter what, if any, faith motivates them. 'The Isaiah Agenda is the bottom-line human right. It provides an adequate basis which human beings, individually and corporately, can build on happiness, freedom and community. The Isaiah Agenda provides the common denominator for our communication. It acknowledges that we sin and are sinned against, it provides a spirit of true partnership with all those who seek the common Isaiah goal.'

This does not mean that we are reduced to a 'do-gooders' club. Fung goes on:

> In the course of our daily involvement with others in the Isaiah Agenda, and in the more heightened occasions of corporate worship, there must come moments when some of our partners stand poised, ready to express an awakened personal faith in Jesus Christ. When such moments arrive, Christians do not hesitate to issue an invitation to discipleship. It could happen in a face-to-face encounter. It could be an altar call. It could be a summons to Eucharist. It could be an announcement of a class for those seeking baptism.

> When such moments come, invite the Christians must.

Through whatever appropriate means, Christians communicate clearly to our Isaiah Agenda partners, 'You are invited to be a disciple of Jesus Christ'.

Such moments may not come for some or many of our partners. Then the Christians wait and continue to work the Isaiah Agenda with our partners and continue to worship God.

If we have no links with the common Isaiah Agenda then our communication channels with the world become terribly narrow and our fishing expeditions take place in heavenly waters that have no earthly use!

The place of dialogue in communication

The world has altered significantly in its religious allegiance. If present trends continued, the Church of the year 2000 would effectively be a Church where the Africans, Asians and South American peoples would play a major leadership role. The Church of the West would need to come to terms with these changes. It would need to be transformed in such a way that it could be enabled to give over its powers of management, leadership and control, and yet have the graciousness of providing the resources and skills to enhance the life of the Communion. Our partnership would be seriously tested as this power-sharing took place. If it did not take place we should not be representative of who we really are.

The Churches of Asia and Africa, in particular, are constantly faced with the claims made by the other living faiths of Islam, Buddhism, Hinduism etc. Evangelism in this context demands extensive interaction between the evangeliser and the evangelised. This interaction needs to take place with other cultures and allegiances that claim the human spirit for their own.

This dialogue would demand a change from us as well, not in terms of our relationship with Christ, but in the structures of dogma, tradition and church paraphernalia that we often confuse with the truth.

Dr M.M. Thomas in his challenging style makes this comment on the Church in India:

> I dimly see the vision of an Indian Christian Church not an Indian Christian Community. It will be Church every day dying for India, and ceasing its existence every now and then, and from the ruins, again resurrecting, only to die the next

77

day, until India is in the Kingdom of God. When that is achieved, we shall not need a Church, for the whole of India will be Christ's body. People tell me, true and apostolic Churches will never become extinct. I do not call such, Christ's Church. There cannot be a true Church with a continuity of existence in the world. It is a contradiction in terms. Die and get resurrected—every day a new fellowship—a new creation—not the old one continuing. That alone can be Christ's Church.

Christianity is not a new system of religion; it is not a new community; it is not a new organisation; and it is not a new nation; it is essentially and fundamentally a new creation with a new spirit realising Christ and His life in the old organisations and in the old nations.

The Church's one foundation is its adventurous faith, that the centre of Universe is the Christ; an impatient dreamer dreaming the Kingdom of God on earth, a youth seeing a vision of redeemed humanity, an adventurer venturing forth to do and to endure with a faith broken but triumphant, a heart bleeding but saving, and a love crucified but embracing.

In all our efforts in dialogue we cannot lay aside the truth that God in Christ has been present and active in all nations, cultures and religions, nor can we lay aside our call to be fishers of women and men.

As Fung reminds us, 'Christian discipleship is a matter of fundamental importance to a person. It affects being, value and relationships. A person has the right to a personal invitation from Jesus Christ or those who purport to speak in his name. No general issued invitation will do. An open-door does not suffice. There has to be an invitation.'

We have the general goal of co-operating in, and for, the common good, and being part of the community that listens and learns, and yet paradoxically we are a community that must proclaim. We must be sellers—fishers for the one who has redeemed us.

Distorted messages

As we move in the market place seeking to promote the Gospel, we must be aware of the distortions that take place in communication; remember the serpent in the Garden of Eden!

Margaret Mulgan, the New Zealand Human Rights Commissioner, tells of her experience in seeking to obtain advice from a communications expert on a particular programme that her department had put together to combat racism. The consultant came back with the advice that he could easily promote the programme, provided she kept the essential message out.

There is always the danger of the bargain basement approach—of providing cheap grace—of falling prey to a 'crossless' Gospel. The market place, we must remember, is a highly competitive environment. Here the customers are sought after with various techniques, not because they are loved, but because they are sales targets to be manipulated and finally trapped into purchase. After which they could well be forgotten: the scalp-hunting communications method.

There is a cacophony of voices, with each one seeking to outdo the other. Real listening can often be lost in the market place as one seeks to provide the bargains, the sales gimmicks, the sales promotions, the cheap options, in order to get a quick sale. It can move into a philosophy that offers you the best for the least. The competition becomes so hard in the market place that some go on the offensive with aggressive marketing. Here all the other products are subject to contempt and ridicule. My product takes on a super glow!

Yes, the market place of the twentieth century is no different from the first century. It can be equally hard and unyielding, and it can provide the quick solution and the easy compromise. As we shift gear from maintenance to mission, we need to be aware of the dangers in the market place and remember that it was the profiteers in religion who finally took Christ to the cross. We are not in the business of communicating the Gospel for cheap popularity, for big business or for putting a million pounds into the kitty. We are in it because we are compelled by the love of God in Christ.

Communicating today

How then do we communicate the Gospel for our times? How do we stand true to our model of Church life firmly based on the incarnation? How do we enter the market place and not fall prey to its traps?

It has been said that who we listen to determines what we hear, where we stand determines what we see, and what we do in response to what we know determines who we really are.

The laity of our Church are at the cutting edge and must enable us to hear, see and act.

COMPASSION AND JUSTICE

We must build up confidence in all the baptized community, so that we become open and willing to share with others in the community in building up the Isaiah vision. Remember that the voice that God speaks most clearly through in modern society is the one that delivers messages of compassion and justice.

The Church, the Body of Christ, becomes visible when it seeks out, acknowledges, and responds with compassion to any and every human need. Its witness is declared openly when it speaks on behalf of, and with, those who suffer injustice.

Two years ago an international research organisation did a world-wide survey on leaders who make a difference in the news, and whom you cannot ignore. The two leading figures in this survey were not the presidents of the superpowers, but a wizened old nun from Albania, Mother Teresa, and an impish cleric from Southern Africa, Archbishop Desmond Tutu. Compassion and justice form a language the world understands.

Compassion and justice for Mother Earth is of intense concern in the world today. I remember being in a primary school in New Zealand a few years ago and asking the kids a common enough question: What do you want to be when you grow up? I was shocked by two responses from these seven-year-olds. 'Nothing,' said one, 'the bomb would have got me.' Another said, 'The ozone hole would have eaten me up, so I won't be around, will I?'

The repair of the earth is a vital justice issue that needs the 'Evangel' of hope. The horror of AIDS is another area that demands the Evangel. It is not a matter for legislation or moral judgement but a call for compassionate action. Compassion, justice: each local Church and Christian can communicate this gospel.

SHARING FAITH

We must encourage each person to recall and remember their faith story and how it relates to the Bible and to their local Church. We must enable our people to break out of the Christian comfort cycle into the hard everyday world, and encourage the sharing of our faith in a natural and easy way.

> One meets Christians who are envious of others or who waste years of wishing they were different and that they had the gifts of somebody else. One meets shy men and women who

wish they were extroverts. But God made shy men and women and chose shy men and women because he wants other shy men and women brought to faith and they might well be put off by the cheerful extrovert with his powerful presentations and glib explanations. God's sovereignty extends to the kind of people we are by disposition and we need to give this back to him for him to perfect. (Michael Griffiths)

I have never found faith-sharing easy, but in God's grace it is possible. I have become a hitch-hiker evangelist! Tripping round the Diocese, it is good to pick up other travellers; usually they are young and have a great deal of questions. Recently, on my way back from a parish, I picked up a huge hulk of a man. He had been surfing. Seeing my collar, his opening comment was 'Huh, you a religious funny, eh!' He was keen on denouncing Christians as hypocrites. His name was Paul and I asked him if he knew after whom he was named. His description of the saint would not fit a textbook: 'Paul was the dude who wasted the Christians.' We got chatting and he wanted to know how I came to faith. No blazing lights for me: a quiet conviction, a growing awareness, a constant stirring of the heart and mind. As we were entering Hamilton, he asked me to stop the car and said to me, 'Do you think this dude Jesus can help me?' I assured him of Christ's love and power, and asked him to allow Jesus to control his life. I don't know what happened to Paul. An opportunity was afforded to proclaim the message and to give an invitation to join the faith community.

I am still in the process of learning to share my faith better.

THE SMALL GROUP

We must enable faith-sharing within small groups. We cannot expect people to go out into the community at large to share their faith if they have not had opportunities to share it within the local church. One of the things I discovered when I went on that trek through the Methodist parishes in New Zealand was the number of faith stories that had never been heard before in the congregation. People had sat next to each other for years and yet never shared their faith journeys.

The telling of stories creates bridges. Paul Simon in his 'Sounds of Silence' wrote:

People talking without speaking,
People hearing without listening,
People writing songs that voices never share,
No-one dared
Disturb the sound of Silence.

Is this the silence that we experience in our churches?

LEVELS OF COMMUNICATION

It is said that there are five levels of communication.

Level 1: 'How are you?'—The supermarket counter level.

This level of communication is more often than not a lack of communication. It is shallow and we don't expect an honest answer. If we got one we would be astounded. It is the conversation of the party or club. There is no real sharing of persons; it is much more pretending.

Level 2: 'Have you heard about . . .?'

At this level, we shelter behind the facts about others, reports and gossip. This is not real communication person to person. We give nothing of ourselves and invite nothing of others.

Level 3: 'In my opinion . . .'

At this level we are willing to take the risk of telling somebody about our ideas, judgements and decisions. But if they disagree or show signs of opposition, we are likely to retreat to safer ground, run for the cover of silence or change the subject. Sermons of a deductive nature fall into these three categories.

Level 4: 'I feel . . .'

Real communication is more than having opinions (Level 3). If you really want someone to know you, then you must tell them about your feelings, head and heart.

Level 5: 'May I remove my mask?'

If we are to have a trusting friendship with others strong enough to share the Gospel, it will need to be based on love, openness and honesty.

It is not surprising that all the bishops who attended the Lambeth Conference found the Bible study groups the most important of all that went on. Why? The group enabled a Level 5 communication.

If we are serious about communication, then Level 5 must be present in our church community.

WORSHIP

We must provide warmth and acceptance in worship that allows for people to acknowledge God at work in their lives.

Worship should free us to communicate with God, with each other, and with our world. There is a danger that what actually takes place is that we feel guilty at not sharing, or we are fearful for not confessing, and then we go out to tell the good news. Instead we share our guilt and fear. Worship should motivate us to communicate honestly with no masks on. Worship should allow for positive ritual, custom and tradition in both the corporate life of the congregation and in individual lives. It must hold to the beauty of the past, but its heart must beat the rhythm of our times.

One of the most positive gatherings for young people that I have been a regular part of is the camp run over the Easter period from Maundy Thursday through till Easter Day. Many of the young people who have had very little connection with the Church find the ancient rituals of the Passover Meal, the Vigil, the Tenebrae, and the waiting for the rising of the sun on Easter Day a most moving experience. In secular culture where negative ritual has become a subtle, destructive influence we must allow for the positive sacramental life of the Church to be portrayed.

PASTORAL MINISTRY

We must be intentional about the pastoral ministry. Our greatest strength in many areas of the world is that people seek us out for the 'maintenance', civic rituals, rites of passage, call them what you will. Baptism, confirmation, marriages, funerals: these are glorious opportunities to stand alongside and provide discussion and faith invitations to those who seek to use the Church in this way. Befriending enables friendship evangelism. And friendship evangelism is still the best and most effective method of bringing people into the community of faith.

SEEKING A COMMON MIND

Structures and models of our decision-making processes, be they synods, councils or conferences, need to reflect a more consultative and caring way of handling conflict and challenge. I am personally not convinced that the parliamentary mode, which is based on the skill of oratory, debate, and division, is an adequate model to deal with the complex issues of ethics and human relationships on which the Church must seek a common mind. Neither does it seem to be a healthy way of discerning the Spirit of Christ in issues of doctrine and ministry. The system tends to polarise us into positions of defence and attack that leave communion shattered and without the witness of the reconciled community.

USING THE MEDIA

We need to provide for creative responses through the available local media on local issues, and learn to use the radio, newspaper and television to proclaim Christ, not as a 'super-telecom' being, but as one who is immersed in the life of people.

DIALOGUE

Lastly, we need to enable Christian apologetics to take its place with the various facets of global culture, and in dialogue with other faiths and ideologies, so that an intelligent and rational challenge is made to the scientific and religious minds of our times.

God works through people

In the end the Gospel communicates not by our skill or by expert methods, or even by the latest technique. We must understand and use the best forms of communication, but ultimately it is God's gift, God's responsibility, God's task. And God works in strange ways and through strange people. It works and changes lives and communities when it is motivated by love and enabled by prayer.

A story is told of a French missionary who had been working among the Moslems for ten years in West Africa. A visitor said to him one day, 'How many converts have you had?'

'Oh, one, two, maybe three.'

'Three converts in ten years! Why do you stay?'

'Why do I stay? Because God put me here.'

Bishop Mortimer Arias of Bolivia says, 'The Gospel is not a possession; it is a stewardship. Nobody can deprive us of this privilege or relieve us from this responsibility.'

God is not in the collecting business, but in the creation business; so we stand with God in that eternal task, knowing that in our weakness God will be strong.

The Decade of Evangelism calls us to the task of communication. May we communicate Christ the Eternal Word in the power of the Spirit, who at creation acted and continues to act, making us new.

Let me close with a story. A communications expert went to heaven (miracles are possible, you know). He sought Christ out for an urgent interview.

'I must ask you this question,' he said. 'The message of God's love healing and making whole, reconciling the world through the love given so freely on the cross, is the most powerful symbol ever conceived. It is truly a divine message. There is however one snag: you have left it in the hands of a terrible mob: Peter, Mary, Martha, John. They just can't deliver; they deny, betray and usually mess things up. You cannot possibly leave it to them. You must have a master plan that leaves out these obvious weak links.'

The Christ was silent for a while, and then said, 'No. I have got only John, Mary, George, Rhoda, Sam, Roger and that mad mob of weak but willing friends. If they do not communicate my faith, hope and love—I have no other plans.'

Section Reports

I. SPIRITUALITY AND JUSTICE

Introduction

We are a group of people, lay and ordained, male and female, from 17 different countries, meeting together to discuss Spirituality and Justice. As the days of meeting have passed, in Bible study, worship and discussion, we have affirmed our common faith in God: Father, Son and Spirit. We have shared stories and personal experiences of human pain and struggles for freedom from oppression and injustice. In so doing we have appreciated the truth of the statement from the Lambeth Conference 1988:

> Shared experience is also shared spirituality, shared
> discovery of a life in Christ.[1]

We have discovered our common commitment to the realisation of peace and justice for all, and to the values of the Kingdom of God in human society. We believe that our work on this topic is vital for the Decade of Evangelism. We have also been enriched by our fellowship as members of the family of Churches of the Anglican Communion. As a contribution to the Decade of Evangelism, we offer our work to the members of the Communion, and beyond it to the wider Christian world.

The task

We have addressed two basic themes. First, the connection between spirituality and justice, which is revealed in Holy Scripture, and is witnessed to in the life and ministry of individual Christians, and corporately through the witness of the Church. Secondly, the relationship between contemplation and action. We asked the question: Is there a dichotomy between the life of prayer and Christian holiness on the one hand, and on the other Christian action which seeks for justice and a resolution of conflict? Are they mutually incompatible, or are they so bound together that one without the other is either mere pietism or outright secularised political agenda?

In preparation for the meeting there were as background three documents. These were : Naim Stifan Ateek, *Justice and only justice*[2]; Colin Craston (ed.), *Open to the Spirit*[3]; and Donal Dorr, *Spirituality and justice*[4]. Each of them was informative and fruitful for the task; and they are commended for study to Anglicans and other Christians who wish to join in the task of discovering the exact nature of the relationship between spirituality and justice.

The Section was challenged in the task by the words of its Chairman, the Revd Canon Winston Ndungane, who expressed his expectations and hopes for the work of our Section as follows:

—A coming into being of a Church that has been led by true prayer to see itself as a remnant called by God to witness to the crucified and risen Lord in a world that needs to experience once more the Christian meaning of death and life.

—Establishing in every Diocese an institute of Christian spirituality.

—An examination in each local situation where the Kingdom has come, is coming and is absent, and to work in a practical way to further the Kingdom.

—A reallocation of staff responsibilities at the ACC in order that one person is set aside as a resource for the promotion of the intrinsic interconnection between spirituality and justice.

—The challenging of the Church by ACC-8, in the light of the· rapid political, economic and social changes that are taking place throughout the world, to take a lead in world events.[5]

The dilemma

Historically, different groups of Christians have emphasised either spirituality or social action. Each has seen other groups as holding an unbalanced or incomplete view of the Gospel and Gospel ministry. Some have said that others have no interest in evangelism and little interest in the nurturing of Christians to a mature faith in Christ, and that they are really social activists. Others have accused their fellows of being remote from the concerns of this world, lacking any social dimension in their ministry, and uninterested in the plight of victims of hunger, poverty, violence and oppression. This, they say, displays no understanding of the teaching of Scripture or appreciation of the ministry and witness of the people of God through the ages.

Yet a review of the history of the Church, and the Anglican Communion in particular, will produce a crowded witness of

Christians whose commitment to an evangelistic, teaching and pastoral ministry has been accompanied by a robust ministry to the social needs of their age.

The conclusion is inescapable that, for the Christian, spirituality and justice are interconnected, each being incomplete without the other. How is the link between them demonstrated? This was the question which we addressed.

The method

In a number of meetings we shared together our own understanding of spirituality and justice and the relationship they have in each person's ministry. We found it true that our personal understanding is informed by our particular environment and circumstances, and the issues which are of vital concern to the Churches from which we come. This added a richness and diversity to the discussions from which all benefited.

For this reason our report is also informed by the experience, life situation and concerns of each of the members of our group. We need to understand each other. We need to see the way our separate understandings of the Christian faith are informed by our cultural heritage and political and socio-economic environment. We take this to be a part of the heritage of our Anglican family and an aspect of the fellowship that we share in this Communion.

The major task is to define spirituality and the distinctiveness of Christian spirituality. However, before entering into that issue, the report must focus on questions which were raised in group discussion. These are: Is there a natural spirituality? And how should the spirituality of other faiths be approached?

Is there a 'natural spirituality'?

When this question was posed, we found it to be fundamental. Is there a spirituality to be found in every human person? Reflection led us to answer, 'Yes.' We are all conscious of the spirituality of indigenous peoples in every nation, a spirituality which is often denied or disdained. Yet do we not have in such spiritualities an expression of that search for the transcendent, that innate consciousness of an 'otherness' which all human beings possess? This is both an aspect of the image of God in every person, and also a testimony to the sense of relationship with the Creator which everyone has.

One member of the group shared with us that he had always understood spirituality to be 'religious practice', until his ministry brought him into contact with the North American Indian people, who taught him that spirituality is about the whole of life, that life itself is an expression of spirituality, and that it is corporate and not simply individual. In African traditional religions, and in ancient Eastern religions, the whole of life is viewed as spiritual, and justice is a natural consequence of this. Insights of this kind broaden our vision, and remind us that we do not 'take God' to human beings when we approach them in our Christian ministry. We find God already there before us, having prepared the way, and inviting us to share in his mission in the world.

> For what can be known about God is plain to them, because God has shown it to them. Ever since the creation of the world his invisible nature, namely, his eternal power and deity, has been clearly perceived in the things that have been made. (Rom 1.19-20, *RSV*)

The spirituality of other faiths

Some of our members, who live in a context where Christians are a minority surrounded by a majority of people of other faiths, reminded us of the importance of noting the spirituality of other religions. We recognise this, and also that others sincerely long for God. Spirituality is common to all religions of the world, for all have a spirituality distinctive to their own understanding of the divine dimension in the universe and in human life. In Christian understanding this phenomenon is again evidence of the image of the Creator in human beings. There is a human yearning for relationship with God.

Undoubtedly there are common features to be found in all spiritualities, however varied in form and style. A realisation of this will show that it is short-sighted to limit consideration of spirituality to one's own religious tradition. So Christians can learn from contact with other spiritualities.

We found the report of the Dogmatic and Pastoral Concerns section of the Lambeth Conference 1988 helpful in regard to this question. We agree that we may have to correct our particular expression of the Christian faith in the light of the commitment of non-Christians, and that we may not yet have even heard of the questions which they are struggling to answer in their particular contexts. We also agree that 'there seems to be no reason to break the long tradition of the majority of Christian apologists in affirming what we can in the deep commitments of our non-Christian neighbours.'[6] It is our hope that Anglicans will continue to search for a deeper understanding of the things of God, calling upon the insights of the many traditions, cultures and languages in which the Churches of the Communion are to be found.[7]

We also found the question of other faiths pertinent to our consideration of justice and spirituality. We noted the report of ACC-6[8], and we agree that Christians must serve and act on behalf of those in need and those who are victims, of whatever circumstance. Whenever possible this should be done in co-operation with, as well as on behalf of, people of other faiths.

In spite of all that we have affirmed above, some of us would find it hard to agree with the proposition that other religions and spiritualities are alternative paths to God.

What is spirituality?

Many definitions of this term were presented in the group discussion: 'Spirituality is the acceptance of the Kingdom of God in my life, it is a daily consciousness of the presence of God in my life.' 'Spirituality is the possessing of the Holy Spirit in someone, having godliness and holiness of living in an individual.' 'In India spirituality commences from the earliest days of one's life in the home. It broadens as one's experience of life grows, and especially as one meets other faiths. It has to do with religion, liturgy, worship and devotion.' 'There is no legitimate Christian spirituality unless it is incorporated into true "body of Christ" spirituality. One measurement of spirituality is in the quality of relationship with others, that is, justice, which is the activity of the law of love.' 'Spirituality includes love of God and fear of God. For eastern peoples it is learnt through the family where self-sacrificing love is modelled by parents for their children. In the family one also learns about fear, which includes respect and trust. The sacraments help us to build our spirituality.' 'Spirituality is the product of the working of God in and through me. It is reinforced through public and private devotion.' 'In my country spirituality comes from the community, not from private spirituality. Our life is always together in community. We emphasize integration in the face of diversity and conflict.'

Such was the diversity of our opinion and experience. And yet we found ourselves in agreement, that spirituality is not to be viewed simply as a matter of religious practice, concerned with the personal life of prayer, holiness and perhaps asceticism, and expressed publicly through the liturgical and sacramental life of the community of Christians in the Church. It certainly covers those activities, yet we are agreed that the fundamental notion behind spirituality is the idea of *relationship.*

Spirituality is the link between God and his children. It is a relationship which is mutual and reciprocal. God seeks it because of his love for his children; we seek it because of our need, because of our sense of restlessness and incompleteness without that relationship with the Creator God who made us: in Augustine's words, 'Our hearts are restless till they find their rest in thee.'

This relationship is expressed personally through prayer and Bible reading, through devotional practices based on a perception of the presence of God in one's life, and a desire to grow more fully aware of that presence and to live in harmony with the will and purposes of God. The relationship is expressed corporately through the devotional and liturgical life of the community of faith, and through united action in the name and for the sake of the Creator.

Yet the relationship is prior to the devotional practice, and the devotional practice serves to deepen and strengthen the relationship. The devotional practice, both private and public, is mere empty form unless it is empowered by the relationship with God.

While we stress the need for the personal aspect of spirituality, 'my relationship with God', we must avoid remaining only with a private expression of that spirituality. Our spirituality must touch every aspect of our lives, our personal relationships with God, our relationships with other people, and our life in community and society. It is in this area that we shall later demonstrate the connection between spirituality and justice.

Christian spirituality

What is it that makes Christian spirituality distinctive? It cannot be the particular devotional practices of Christians, for they are in many instances matched by devotional practices in other faiths. It is not unique to Christianity to pray, to study the Scriptures, to meditate, to fast, to listen to and obey the teacher etc.

What is unique to Christian spirituality is the relationship which informs it. For the Christian is related to the God who is the Father who loves, and who sent his Son into the world to live and 'to serve, and to give his life as a ransom for many' (Mark 10.45; John 3.16). The Christian is related to the God who is the reconciling God, who through the death and resurrection of Christ reconciles women and men to himself (2 Cor 5.18ff), restores hostile and divided human relationships (Eph 2.11-18), and reconciles the whole created order to himself (Col 1.20). The Christian is related to the God who is peace (Heb 13.20; Rom 15.33) and to the God of justice (Isa 30.18). The Christian is related to the God who is Trinity, for the Father gives love, the Son bestows grace, and the Spirit imparts fellowship (2 Cor 13.14).

Love, peace, reconciliation, justice, service are characteristics of the life of those whose spirituality derives from relationship with this God, who is the Father of Jesus Christ. This is the uniqueness of Christian spirituality, that it is marked by relationship with God in Jesus Christ, and illuminated by the work of the Holy Spirit. The specific and unique standing of the Christian is to be 'in Christ'. That concept, expressed so often in the New Testament, determines what Christian spirituality is. The Christian believer, baptized into Christ, lives by the redeeming and regenerating grace of God given in Christ crucified and risen, received in faith and through the indwelling Spirit of God. Christian spirituality is essentially a growth in this particular relationship with God: Father, Son and Holy Spirit. This relationship alone can motivate a person sufficiently to engage actively in all God's purposes in the world.

There are various patterns of 'spirituality', that is, differing forms of liturgical and devotional practice both public and private, known in Anglicanism. Yet their authenticity comes, not through the fact that they are Anglican, but only as they are expressive of this relationship with God, known to all who are baptized into Christ.

In genuine Christian spirituality, there are spiritual devotion and practice and, at the same time, relationships and a life in the world which bear the stamp of the God who is saviour, strengthener, reconciler and giver of peace and justice. This is illustrated by the following comment upon the life and witness of the Church of the Province of Southern Africa:

> Where renewal has been genuine, there has come about a deepened spirituality, a mature faith and an equipping for service as God's instruments for the urgent and pressing task of bringing about God's justice in a polarised South Africa. The renewal holds both the possibility and the power for equipping the Church for authentic Christian witness and the ministry of reconciliation in a strife-torn and divided

South Africa. A Church that is truly renewed is one which is a
source of renewal within the community.[9]

A comment in similar vein, which saw in spirituality the motivating
factor in action for justice, was made by a member of our group who
spoke from experience of the civil rights movement in the United
States:

> It was clear that the oppressors and the oppressed had
> different working definitions of spirituality and justice. For
> us who are black people in America, spirituality was carved
> out of a mountain of despair. It was only an unshakeable
> faith, that God was always in control and always on the side
> of the oppressed, which saw us through and sustained us in
> our quest for justice in a land of injustice. This knowledge
> came through our awareness of the presence of God in our
> lives. It is no accident that the civil rights leaders all came
> from the black Church.

Justice

Many definitions of this term were presented in the group discussion:
'Justice is the equitable administration of the law so that no one is
demeaned or demoralised in the process.' 'Justice is the way God
looks at life, it is the activity of God in the world in every aspect of
life.' 'Justice includes respect for humanity, and injustice is the denial
of what is due to a person.' 'Spirituality is directly related to justice,
which is the ordering of affairs in society.' 'Spirituality is relationship
with God, and justice is the working out of this relationship with God
in relationships with others.' 'In India justice is to do with the law of
the land, it is not to do with morality in our situation. There is a
dichotomy between law and morality, and religion looks to the law
courts for justice. There is therefore underlying tension for us between
the idea of justice which springs out of our spirituality, and that justice
which actually exists.'

When we consider justice in relation to spirituality, the justice to
which we refer is not the justice of legalism and the law court, of law as
made by human beings, but the justice demanded by Scripture. For a
Christian, the law is the commandment to love God and neighbour.
Justice and injustice are measured by our success and failure in
fulfilling that law. The law of love demands that no person, by her or
his own way of life or exercise of influence, should deface the image of
God in others by, for example, denying them a basic freedom, or food,

clothing, shelter, education, health care or employment.[10]

Any discussion of justice is deficient if it refers solely to personal justice and its corollary, injustice, confining the terms to matters of relationship between individuals and groups of persons and their just or unjust actions and attitudes towards each other. Alongside that understanding of justice must be placed an understanding of injustice which accepts that it can be found built into the institutions and structures of a society in such a way that their very existence and operation result in permanent injustice and oppression.

This structural injustice may have no relation at all to the personal attitudes and morality of those who service or administer the institution. Indeed they may individually be people who are morally upright and of great personal integrity, and the Church also has a pastoral responsibility to them. The fault is not in the individual, but is intrinsic to the nature of the institution or structure itself. This area of structural injustice which reinforces and maintains a system of oppression and violence, or a cycle of poverty, can rarely be broken through by the victim of the injustice. The system or institution itself must be challenged and changed. It is here that Christian social concern must be found to be most active. The Church cannot rest comfortably alongside institutions and systems which by their very nature are causing people to suffer and to be deprived of basic human rights. The Church must challenge and act for change and transformation in the name of the God of justice. At the same time, the Church must be prepared to challenge injustice within her own institutions and structures. This is part of the cost of following the way of Christ. One example of such a situation in the West Indies was presented to the group.

> The Caribbean today is the product of colonisation, which involved structural injustice and a two-tiered structure of society. That is, there were the privileged and powerful (and the Anglicans were to be found in this group), and there were the oppressed, who were poor and powerless. Slavery existed in this society. The colonial period has ended, but its legacy remains. The powerful, a small minority, still control the wealth and institutions of the society, and the majority of the people are still the poor and the oppressed. This structural injustice includes a lack of opportunity for education and employment. My spirituality impels me to work for justice, for equality of opportunity for all.

Christian spirituality and justice

We have indicated in a number of places that we believe that the connection between spirituality and justice is grounded in the very nature of God. An exploration of this, and the consequent demand upon individuals and Churches to act justly, should be based upon that understanding of God which we find revealed in Scripture. A report of this kind is not the place to develop a fully-fledged biblical theology of spirituality and justice, but we should indicate something of the biblical background that has informed our discussion.

The God whose self-revelation came to the people of Israel was clearly a holy God, who demanded holiness of life from the people (Isa 6.3; Lev 11.44). God was also a God of justice, who loved justice, was just in all his ways, and demanded just living and just actions from the people (Isa 30.18; Ps 37.28; 145.17; Isa 1.17; Jer 22.3; Amos 5.24). At the same time God was experienced as a God of righteousness (Jer 22.3), of mercy (Ps 25.6; Lam 3.22), of compassion (Ps 145.9) and of love (Jer 31.3; Lam 3.22). Above all, this holy and just God was experienced as a saviour (Isa 54.8; 49.26; Ps 106.21). God also abhors injustice, and acts on behalf of those who are victims. God intercedes for them and pleads their cause (Prov 22.22-23). God extends divine protection to all who suffer oppression and injustice, and condemns the oppressors (Isa 10.1-2). God is the saviour of the oppressed (see Ps 76.8-9).

These aspects of the character of God must be reflected in the life of his people. That is the sign and witness of their relationship with the God of the covenant, who is steadfast in all his ways. The prophetic call to the people of God to return to a life characterised by justice, love, righteousness, mercy and compassion is a call to return to the faithful relationship with the God of Israel, the God of the covenant, who saves his people.

It is therefore in this prophetic call that we find the clue to the relationship between spirituality and justice. The relationship with the God revealed in Scripture requires an outworking of that relationship in the life of the Christian believer. The actions which demonstrate the character of God, however they are marked by our human frailty and sin, are signs of the Kingdom, visibly evident in the life of the Christian, and they call attention, not to the individual person, but to the God who is served. The other side of this is that unjust actions and lack of mercy, compassion and righteousness are denials of the character of God, with the result that people turn away, not only from the believer but from God.

The words of the prophet Micah have been an important focal point for our discussions:
>   This is what Yahweh asks of you:
>   only this, to act justly,
>   to love tenderly
>   and to walk humbly with your God.   (Micah 6.8, *JB*)

We accept the thesis of Donal Dorr[11] that the three demands made by the Lord in this text provide the basis for a balanced spirituality.

'To love tenderly' is an aspect of our interpersonal relationships, and it requires us to treat everybody with respect and gentleness, and with the dignity that is due to them as children of the Creator. This demand upon us requires us to be other-centred, genuinely interested in and caring for other people. It requires us to trust ourselves to others, to allow ourselves to become vulnerable, to be willing to risk even rejection and hurt. This demand also requires us to be faithful in our relationships, as God is faithful to his word and promise.

'To walk humbly with God' refers to the personal relationship which is God's gift of grace to each believer. This is the basis of our spirituality. This relationship is experienced daily as the Holy Spirit leads through the daily events of life, enabling obstacles to be overcome which contain in themselves opportunities for growth and holiness, and strengthening into that growth which leads to full humanity as a person of the Kingdom, as Jesus was. It requires a sense of having experienced forgiveness, of being loved and accepted in spite of weakness, faithlessness and sin (see the parable of the Pharisee and the tax-collector in Luke 18). It requires, too, an acceptance of the Lordship of Christ, not only in the personal life but over the whole of human history. It requires commitment to the values of the Kingdom of God, and it is at this point that this demand to 'walk humbly with God' intersects with the demand 'to act justly'.

'To act justly' takes us out of the sphere of interpersonal relationships into the public and political sphere. Justice has to characterise the way a community and society is organised, so that wealth, power, privilege, rights and responsibilities are shared equally by all. In recent decades it has been recognised in Christian writing and theology that the struggle to bring justice into each society requires a working out of the 'option for the poor' that is to be found clearly in Scripture. The powerful and the wealthy have the resources to care for themselves, but the poor need the special protection of society, and especially of the community of believers. A prophetic spirituality, that is, the demand 'to act justly', will require a challenge to the existing order on behalf of those who are poor and oppressed and victims, and it will seek the radical changes that social justice will demand in the particular situation.

In the Gospels Jesus demonstrated a similar care for the poor, the hungry, the sinners, those who were the outcasts of society. We observe that he took the teaching of Isaiah (Isa 61.1-8) and applied it to his own ministry and mission, in the sermon preached in the synagogue at Nazareth (Luke 4.16-21). The Sermon on the Plain sets a prophetic agenda for the people of God (e.g. Luke 6.20-36), and in the Epistles the demand for holiness of life and social concern is set out (Rom 12.6-21; Col 3.12-15; and compare 1 Peter 1.15ff).

God calls us to love, mercy, compassion, righteousness, holiness and justice in word and in deed. It is imperative that each individual Christian and each community of believers work out the implications of this call in their own environment, and having reflected upon it, move into activity in the name of the God of justice and holiness.

Justice and governments

Although it is a biblical concept that governments and leaders are ordained by God to ensure that justice is maintained in society and nation, they themselves also need to be kept in check, or otherwise they may go beyond the prescribed limits of their authority, thus becoming oppressive. When this happens, or even before it happens, the Church should come into the picture, empowered by her prophetic role, so that the situation is corrected. The Church is to act to bring liberation to the oppressed. This is the most difficult aspect of the Christian ministry, especially where Christian values of spirituality and justice are not followed and practised in the society at large. (See Rom 13.1-7; Deut 16.18-20.)

In every political system, whether multi-party or single-party, the Church, both inside and outside the party system, must speak on behalf of the weak, the voiceless, the poor and the oppressed. (See Amos 3.7-11.)

Prayer and justice

There are many people who would see prayer and action as alternatives open to the Christian. In the integrated vision of spirituality and justice this is not so, for they are interconnected. There must be a passionate commitment to both prayer and social action. Action for justice is only truly Christian when it springs out of a trust and confidence in the providential purposes of the God of justice and mercy. This trust and confidence is expressed in the desire of the Christian to pray, to converse with God and to listen to God in order to seek his mind and his will. A prophetic vision born out of Christian spirituality will not allow us to substitute prayer for action. Nor will it allow us to engage in action for justice which is not prayerful, which is not combined with a willingness to turn to God for guidance, for if we do that we rely upon our own efforts apart from the God of justice.

Jesus is our model. He never failed to pray, to draw aside to commune with the Father, to seek his will. Some may say that we do not need to pray, since Jesus taught us that the Father knows our need, even before we ask (Matt 6.8), but we pray to indicate our trust in the mercy and purpose and power of God, and we make explicit that attitude of trust and petition which should permeate the life of the Christian (Matt 7.7-8). Jesus also taught that we should pray to the Father to bring the Kingdom and Kingdom values to our own life and society (Matt 6.9-10). Anyone who wishes to live according to the example and teaching of Jesus will pray constantly, for this is true Christian spirituality. The prayer of Jesus in the Garden of Gethsemane is a prayer of freedom. 'Not my will but yours be done.' This model of prayer and reliance on the purposes and will of God will free us from the temptation to rely on our own effort and our own programmes and desires when we are 'acting justly'. We draw attention to Resolution 71 of the Lambeth Conference 1988:

> This Conference calls upon individuals, prayer groups, congregations, devotional organisations, and Religious Communities to give renewed emphasis to the work of prayer. We call upon the bishops of the Anglican Communion to give a strong lead in the ministry of prayer in all its forms, so that we may know God's will for our time and be empowered for the mission of the Lord Jesus Christ.[12]

Issues of justice

Many issues of human rights and justice were discussed by the group. They were not an exhaustive list of justice issues across the world, for they arose from the experience of the members. Nor were they able to be treated in depth. We also reminded ourselves of the danger of confronting issues of justice without fully understanding every side of the question, for often the Church loses credibility in her zeal for justice, because of failure to undertake the proper 'homework' before making sweeping statements and pronouncements. In spite of this reminder, there are crucial issues which must be confronted and addressed by the world and the Church community. We draw a number of issues to the attention of ACC-8 and of the Anglican Communion, recommending that they be studied in depth, that this work be shared throughout the Communion and with our ecumenical partners, and where necessary acted upon appropriately. We present these issues in the form of an extended resolution presented by our Section to ACC-8. See Resolution 3 on pages 157-158 below.

Practical outcomes

It is our belief that the content of this Section report should be communicated through the inter-Anglican secretariat to the member Churches of the Communion, so that they may in turn refer it to Dioceses and local congregations. We would hope that these issues might be raised in clergy training, and that educational material might be prepared which could be used to raise them throughout the membership of the Communion. We are concerned that the fruit of our discussion should not remain simply with those who were involved in it, but that it might be of benefit to the entire Communion. We suggest that local, regional and provincial committees might be set up as appropriate, if they are not already in existence, to promote and educate Church people on issues of spirituality and justice.

We agree with the Section Chairman that the setting up of diocesan centres for spirituality and justice would assist in the promotion of these concerns throughout the member Churches.

We understand the circumstances which have led to a failure to provide a report from the Peace and Justice Network to ACC-8, but would hope that such reports will be made to future meetings of the ACC. We are unanimous in the hope that ACC staff resources will be reallocated so that the spirituality and justice portfolio can be serviced.

The promise of grace

In this report we have demonstrated the intrinsic interconnection between spirituality and justice. We have shown that an authentic Christian spirituality is not only God-centred and biblically based, but also that it manifests itself in acts of justice in the world. We have urged members of the Anglican Communion to a life of prayer that is persistent, penetrative and productive. At the same time we have called them to a life of service and action that flows from a deepened relationship with God. As we stated in our Introduction, we believe our work has important relevance to the Decade of Evangelism.

In an unjust world this Christian service of which we write includes speaking and acting on behalf of the weak, the voiceless, the poor and the oppressed. For we recognise that none of us is truly free until all of us 'no longer swelter in the heat of injustice', whatever its form.

We recognise our frailty and inability to do what is good. However, we are encouraged by this word of promise:

> My grace is sufficient for you, for my power is made perfect in weakness. (2 Cor 12.9, *RSV*)

REFERENCES

1   *The truth shall make you free.* The Lambeth Conference 1988, p 86
2   Naim Stifan Ateek, *Justice and only justice* (Orbis Books, New York, 1989)
3   Colin Craston (ed.), *Open to the Spirit* (Anglican Consultative Council, London, 1987)
4   Donal Dorr, *Spirituality and justice* (Gill and Macmillan, Dublin, 1984)
5   *Anglican information,* June 1990, p 4
6   *The truth shall make you free,* p 94
7   ibid.
8   *Bonds of affection* (Anglican Consultative Council, London, 1984), pp 85-86
9   Winston Ndungane, 'An evaluation of charismatic renewal within the Church of the Province of Southern Africa' in Craston (ed.), *Open to the Spirit,* p 37
10 A full discussion of human rights is found in the Report of ACC-4 (London, Ontario, 1979), pp 28-40. Study of this discussion is recommended.
11 Donal Dorr, *Spirituality and justice*
12 *The truth shall make you free,* p 239

II.   MISSION, CULTURE AND HUMAN DEVELOPMENT

We have taken mission as the central co-ordinating theme of our Section, and have approached the other subjects (human development, liturgy and culture) from the perspective of the missionary imperative. We have in effect asked: How do these topics relate to the whole mission of the Church as ACC and the Anglican Communion understand it? We believe this approach has been fruitful.

We have also spent time discussing the difficulties in inter-Anglican relationships from a perspective of mission. Our work in this area, however, has been passed on to the special group considering identity and authority in the Anglican Communion, and is covered by their report.

Human development in mission

We seek to bring up to date the definition of mission which has been developing within ACC, and to relate that to the current phase of human history. We see this as building on the consistent work done by ACC over many years, relating it to the new situation we now face.

MISSION

There has been a consistent view of mission repeated by ACC, the Lambeth Conference, the Primates' Meeting and others in recent years, which defines mission in a four-fold way:

The mission of the Church is:

(a) to *proclaim the good news* of the Kingdom;
(b) to teach, baptize and *nurture new believers;*
(c) to *respond to human need* by loving service;
(d) to seek to *transform the unjust structures* of society.

We now feel that our understanding of the ecological crisis, and indeed of the threats to the unity of all creation, mean that we have to add a fifth affirmation:

(e) to strive to *safeguard the integrity of creation* and sustain and renew the life of the earth.

Two important elements of this definition have tended to be particularly stressed within the inter-Anglican structures: (i) The call to the Decade of Evangelism has stressed *proclamation* of the Gospel, but usually this is clearly defined in a way which is related to the other elements of the definition. (ii) The idea of *transformation* has also been developing, and needs to be more widely recognised. ACC-6 used a definition of transformation borrowed from the International Evangelical Consultation on the Nature and Mission of the Church (1983): 'a change from a level of human existence that is less than that envisaged by our Creator, to one in which man is fully human and free to move to a state of wholeness in harmony with God, with fellow human beings and with every aspect of his environment'. The

Lambeth Conference 1988 issued a pastoral letter entitled 'On the Gospel and transformation', which said, 'Some lay stress on inner personal change, others on social and political change. But increasingly, as we have learned from each other and grown in commitment to each other, we have recognised the real task into which Jesus Christ is sending us all. We must hold these varied emphases together in one gospel and one witness in the one Body.'

This concept of transformation can be a corrective to any tendency to isolate evangelism from social responsibility. The Decade of Evangelism must also be a decade of transformation.

HUMAN DEVELOPMENT

Our mission can only be understood, and therefore obediently undertaken, in the *context* of the critical stage of human history at which we stand in the 1990s.

The World Convocation on Justice, Peace and the Integrity of Creation in Seoul, Korea, in March 1990 recognised this and made a number of important affirmations and covenants. We commend the full Seoul document for study, and give here a summary of the main findings:

SUMMARY OF THE SEOUL AFFIRMATIONS

1   All exercise of power is accountable to God. This implies the right of all people to full participation in forms of government and economic structures.
2   God's option for the poor. Christians have a duty to ally themselves with organisations and efforts which are dedicated to achieving the eradication of exploitation and oppression.
3   The equal value of all races and peoples. People of every race, caste and ethnic group are of equal value and reflect the rich plurality of God's creation.
4   Male and female are created in the image of God.
5   Truth is at the foundation of a community of free people. This means that access to truth and education, information and means of communication are basic human rights.
6   The peace of Jesus Christ. The only basis for lasting peace is justice; true peace means every human being dwelling in secure relatedness to God, neighbour, nature and self.
7   The creation as beloved of God. We have a responsibility to care for creation, to respect the rights of future generations and to conserve and work for the integrity of creation.
8   The earth is the Lord's. Human use of land and waters should not destroy the life-giving power of the earth.

II. Mission, culture and human development

9 The dignity and commitment of the younger generation. The rights and needs of the younger generation should be protected.
10 Human rights are given by God. Their protection and promotion are essential for freedom, justice and peace.

The ten affirmations are followed by four covenants, by which Christians and Churches are called upon to commit themselves to work:

SUMMARY OF THE SEOUL COVENANTS

1 For a just economic order at local, national, regional and international levels for all people; for liberation from the bondage of foreign debt that affects the lives of hundreds of millions of people. The Churches should support economic systems and policies that ensure that the dignity of people and creation comes before profit, and make themselves free of complicity with unjust economic structures.
2 For the security of all nations and peoples, for the demilitarisation of international relations, for a culture of non-violence as a force for change and liberation. The Churches should witness to the love of God through, among other things, practising our Lord's call to love the enemy, through giving up any theological or other justification of the use of military power, through developing justice and peace ministries.
3 For preserving the gift of the earth's atmosphere to nurture and sustain the world's life; for building a culture that can live in harmony with creation's integrity; for combatting the causes of destructive changes to the atmosphere which threaten to disrupt the earth's climate and create widespread suffering. The Churches can develop new theological perspectives concerning creation and the place of humanity within it, and join the global, local and personal efforts to safeguard the integrity of creation.
4 For the eradication of racism and discrimination at national and international levels for all peoples. The Churches should take the lead in breaking down walls which divide people because of their ethnic origin, by implementation of such principles in the policies and practices of Churches and Church-related bodies.

These affirmations and covenants should be seen as the beginning of a process opening out to the Christian Churches, congregations and movements, and even further to all people struggling for justice, peace and the integrity of creation. This Act of Covenanting in Seoul constitutes an open invitation to enter into a network of mutual commitment for action.

Section reports

DOXOLOGY

Having committed ourselves in Covenant Solidarity and
Mindful that we are stewards of Creation
We join with all You made
To celebrate Your glory
And to sing Your praise.

Glory to God
Who in the beginning created all things
And saw that it was good.

Glory to Jesus
Firstborn of the new Creation
And Redeemer of all.

Glory to the Spirit
Who in the beginning hovered over the water
And who fills Creation with Your love.

SHAPING AN ANGLICAN RESPONSE

We commend these affirmations and covenants. We affirm not only
the importance of these crucial life-or-death issues, but also that:

 The real danger lies in the interaction of these threats.
 Together they represent a global crisis. Unless far-reaching
 changes are made now the crisis will intensify and may turn
 into a real catastrophe for our children and grand-children.

We therefore affirm these findings (a) as an important call to
covenant commitment on the major interconnected issues of our
time, which are all both local and global, and (b) as a significant step
towards a more integrated Christian witness.

We ask the Churches in the Anglican Communion to accept the
principles of the Seoul covenants, and to identify and take action on
the points which relate to their own urgent local concerns. Not
everyone can or should try to do everything, but all should be helped
to see their local problems as part of a global and potentially fatal
disease, which together we need to diagnose and treat. All start where
they are, but at the same time must relate to others.

We ask that the Anglican Justice and Peace Network should
effectively: (a) monitor the Anglican Communion's serious adherence
to the Seoul covenants; (b) share examples of specific ways in which
these issues are being tackled locally and regionally in different areas,
show how these can be supported, establish what we can learn from

them, and identify what their implications are for our own witness (for example, the Church in Jerusalem led by Bishop Kafity and the Church in South Africa led by Archbishop Tutu are both sacrificially engaged with their own societies, but they have obvious implications for our responsibility in other societies); (c) develop the common historical and theological analysis needed, and thus move towards a common Christian 'confession' on the global crisis; and (d) make recommendations to the Churches for further action through the ACC.

Liturgy in mission and culture

If liturgy is the work of the people of God it is more than church services. Liturgy is more than prayer books and the details of ritual. Liturgy is the vision of a community of the spirit expressed in the form of story and symbol, the two bound together in the climate of prayer.

Authentic Christian liturgy in any age or culture addresses both the past and the future of the worshippers. Christian liturgy depends upon the biblical story which comes to us from the past, but it always anticipates the fullness of God's Kingdom which is complete in the Christ, but not yet complete in the world and in us. This is why Paul says we celebrate the Lord's Supper 'until he comes' (1 Cor 11.26), and it explains the intimate relationship between the Lord's Prayer (with its petition for the coming of the Kingdom) and the act of communion in the classic eucharistic rites.

Christian liturgy, especially the liturgies of Baptism and Eucharist, are models of the Kingdom. We are washed, anointed, embraced and fed in the realm of God's *shalom* as it has been established in Jesus Christ. Such liturgy is learning: it is education in the lifestyle (personal and social) of the Kingdom, but at the levels of intuition and metaphor rather than of the communication of rational thought reduced to concept. We practise the Kingdom in liturgy so that we may become Kingdom people.

The New Testament witnesses to this role of liturgy as a model of God's Kingdom. Paul and James both condemned injustice in the liturgical assembly, in Corinth where selfish members of the community ate and drank in the presence of poorer members who had no food and wine (1 Cor 11.22), and in the community to which James wrote, where a lower-class member was humiliated on account of his poverty (James 2.1-7).

Liturgy as the model of the Kingdom is no substitute for pursuit of the Kingdom in the rest of life. The fruits of the Spirit are the signs of the Kingdom. But liturgy provides the key, the code, continuously stamped on the members of the Body of Christ.

Liturgy is consequently a point where spirituality and justice intersect. It is the point of tension between 'inner' and 'outer' life. Liturgy is also where tradition and mission meet as past and future come together. This double intersection is where these tensions are addressed in prayer, in story, and in symbol, not as an exercise which is an end in itself but for the sake of Christian living: for personal wholeness, for the life of humanity and the world, on the rock of the unchanging Gospel, and for the future of all.

INTERNATIONAL ANGLICAN LITURGICAL CONSULTATIONS

The Council received the report of the third International Anglican Liturgical Consultation held in August 1989 at York, England. It may be helpful to provide a sketch of the history of the Consultations.

The first Consultation met at Boston, Massachusetts, in August 1985, immediately before a congress of the Societas Liturgica. It was composed of a number of Anglican members of the Societas Liturgica, which is the major international and ecumenical association of the liturgical academy. Membership in the first Consultation was restricted to a group of people who agreed among themselves to address questions related to the communion of children. The findings of the Consultation were subsequently published.

The second International Anglican Liturgical Consultation met at Brixen in northern Italy in August 1987, again in conjunction with a congress of the Societas Liturgica. This time the Consultation was open to all Anglican members of the Societas Liturgica who wished to remain in Brixen for its deliberations. The papers of the Consultation were subsequently published as *A kingdom of priests: liturgical formation of the laity* (Alcuin/GROW LS no. 6, 1988).

The third International Anglican Liturgical Consultation met at York in August 1989, also in conjunction with a congress of the Societas Liturgica. The principal subject of discussion was 'inculturation'. The Consultation produced 'Down to earth worship', which was published with a collection of papers presented to the Consultation by a number of its members as *Liturgical inculturation in the Anglican Communion* (Alcuin/GROW LS no. 15, 1990). The Consultation at York also made provision for its successors by producing a set of guidelines which cover the purpose, membership, leadership, and other procedures of what is clearly becoming a continuing body rather than a series of ad hoc meetings. These guidelines were published in *Findings of the third International Anglican Liturgical Consultation* (Grove Books, December 1989).

Canon Donald Gray of Westminster Abbey was convener of the first three Consultations. Professor David Holeton of Trinity College, Toronto, was elected chairman at the York Consultation for four years.

RESPONSE TO THE INTERNATIONAL ANGLICAN LITURGICAL CONSULTATION 1989

The York statement 'Down to earth worship' is seen to be of central importance. We note that it is addressed 'to all those who worship God throughout the Anglican Communion; and for the special consideration of bishops, teachers of liturgy, and members of Liturgical Commissions'. We commend this statement for study and therefore request that it be attached to the Report of this Council, together with the Guidelines. See Appendixes I and II on pages 172-180.

We found the essays in the publication *Liturgical inculturation in the Anglican Communion* to be timely, helpful, and illustrative of the issues raised in the York statement, and commend the book to the Churches for study in the context of their own work of liturgical renewal. The Churches are also asked to send responses and further examples of liturgical inculturation to the Co-ordinator for Liturgy.

We welcome the Guidelines as set out in the findings of the third International Anglican Liturgical Consultation, and believe that the Consultations have a continuing and important role in addressing liturgical issues affecting the Anglican Communion.

CO-ORDINATOR FOR LITURGY

We express our appreciation of the action of the Anglican Church of Canada in enabling the appointment to the ACC staff of the Revd Paul Gibson as part-time Co-ordinator for Liturgy. We note that the Co-ordinator's immediate goals are:

—to identify sources of information on liturgical development in the Communion,

—to collect documents (and eventually other resources perhaps) which illustrate the development of current and future patterns in liturgy in the Communion, especially as they relate to inculturation,

—to work towards a process by which potential leaders in the field of liturgy in parts of the Communion which include developing countries may receive appropriate education and skills,

—to ensure that the expressed concerns of the Council and of the Lambeth Conference in the area of liturgy are addressed.

Resolution 12(b) of ACC-7 called for the offering of encouragement, support and advice to those Provinces which had, as yet, few liturgically trained specialists, whether in the pastoral or the more theological aspects of liturgy, and in some instances the financing of the training of liturgists. The Co-ordinator has begun to explore the ways in which education in the field of liturgy may be fostered more widely. Conversations with missionary societies have begun, and the question of appropriate context is being addressed, i.e., is it as a rule better to bring people of promise to established 'western' centres of learning, or to develop models of liturgical education which could be offered from time to time to groups of people in their own national and cultural contexts? Some members of the Council expressed the opinion that a helpful model might be the visits of a team able to demonstrate and teach. We recognise that each of these alternatives has value and suggest that they be explored further in discussion. We also recognise that expertise in liturgical development requires an historical approach initially, in order to perceive ways in which the tradition can be faithfully adapted, thus allowing authentic inculturation. In order to be free from history one must learn history.

We recommend that the Co-ordinator for Liturgy asks the Churches for information on the availability of resources and training centres for liturgical development.

Supplement: Offerings for worship

The offerings which follow are attempts to express some of our concerns in ways that could be used, as appropriate, by congregations in worship. The Section felt that it was important to offer illustrative material, but feared that, if it were incorporated in the actual Report of ACC-8, there would be a danger, whatever our words of explanation or reservation, that it would be misunderstood as somehow being material officially 'approved' by the Council.

Nevertheless the Council, in receiving this supplementary material, recommended its publication within the Report as a stimulus to local Churches in their own liturgical explorations, and perhaps as a resource that could be freely used and adapted to the context of various cultures. We repeat that it carries no official approval, having been produced with very limited opportunity for reflection and experiment. If the reaction of any in the Church is 'A good idea—but we could do better,' we ask no more. Get on and do it!

A LITANY OF MISSION

This Litany seeks to present simply the five-fold affirmation on mission in the context of worship. *It may be freely adapted or expanded to suit different circumstances and cultures.* In particular the responses (Hallelujah and Kyrie Eleison) may be sung in various cultural settings. In the Section meeting itself, for example, these responses were identified in forms from Zimbabwe, from South India, from Brazil, and from the Russian Orthodox liturgy.

> Jesus prayed, 'As you sent me, so I send them into the world.'
> We give you thanks that you call us to share your mission in your way; that you call us to faith and to proclaim faith.
> *Response:* **Hallelujah** *(sung in appropriate form)*
>
> Jesus prayed, 'That they may be one as we are one—you, Father, in me and I in you.'
> We give you thanks that you call us to share your gift of unity— the unity we see in the Holy Trinity, Father, Son and Spirit; that you call us to love and to proclaim love.
> *Response:* **Hallelujah**
>
> 'God has revealed to us his purpose: to bring all things in the universe into unity in Christ.'
> We give you thanks that you call us to be the sign and the first-fruits of your will for your whole creation; that you call us to hope and to proclaim hope.
> *Response:* **Hallelujah**
>
>
> The mission of the Church is the work of Christ: 'to proclaim the good news of the Kingdom'.
> We confess that we have been slow to speak the good news of life. We pray that you touch our lips with the burning coals of your living word. Lord, hear us ...
> *Response:* **Lord have mercy. Kyrie eleison** *(in appropriate form)*
>
> The mission of the Church is the work of Christ: 'to teach, baptize and nurture new believers'.
> We confess that we have been slow to pass on with patience the riches of the faith. We pray that you guide us to teach aright, and to build up your body in the Church. Lord, hear us ...
> *Response:* **Lord have mercy. Kyrie eleison.**
>
> The mission of the Church is the work of Christ: 'to respond to human need by loving service'.

We confess that we have been slow to recognise you in the needs and sufferings of others. We pray that when you come to us in the unloveable, the despised and the wretched of the earth, we may know it is you. Lord, hear us ...
Response: **Lord have mercy. Kyrie eleison.**

The mission of the Church is the work of Christ: 'to seek to transform the unjust structures of society'.
We confess that we have been afraid to speak the prophetic word of truth to the powers and principalities of our time. We pray for wisdom and courage so that we may lead this new age to repentance, to confession and to transformation. Lord, hear us ...
Response: **Lord have mercy. Kyrie eleison.**

The mission of the Church is the work of Christ: 'to strive to safeguard the integrity of creation, and sustain and renew the life of the earth'.
We confess that we have too easily accepted the benefits of creation without counting the cost of our rape of the earth. We pray that we may learn to deal gently with our world, that we and our children may live. Lord, hear us ...
Response: **Lord have mercy. Kyrie eleison.**

* * *

RAINBOW'S END?

When the dove cannot fly for its oil-clotted pinions;
When the olive branch withers in soil made impure;
When the rainbow corrodes in a rain become acid;
Will the promise still hold, will the earth yet endure?

If nuclear winter assassinates springtime;
If seedtime made barren brings harvest no more;
If day turns to darkness and dusk without dawning;
How long, Lord, how long will the earth yet endure?

When the safety of some means the misery of many;
When the affluent feast on the flesh of the poor;
When debts must be paid through the weeping of children;
Will his mercy remain, will the earth yet endure?

Where the lamp of the Lamb lights our guilt and our gladness;
Where the book of God's judgement at last is unsealed;
Where the clear crystal river of mercy is flowing;
There the tree of life blossoms, the nations are healed.

Kenyon E. Wright

(Possible tune: 'The Rose of Tralee', Irish folk song)

* * *

110

God gave us the glorious rainbow,
The sign and the symbol of love,
The mark of his covenant mercy,
The olive branch borne by the dove.
We clutch in our terror and trembling
This delicate blue crystal ball,
Half drunk with the power of possession,
Half desolate dread it may fall.

Lord, look on our guilt and our yearning,
And teach us the lesson of love,
That heaven is not for our earning,
Your city descends from above.
The Spirit who crafted creation
Now broods o'er our arrogant strife,
And calls us to joy and to suffering:
Choose Christ and not Caesar, choose Life.

Kenyon E. Wright

* * *

A LITANY OF THANKSGIVING

(For possible use at inter-Anglican events)

We are the scattered children of Canterbury, gathered from every colour, tribe and tongue.

We give thanks for our common heritage, for the traditions of worship and order we share, for the stories of yesterday which have become part of our story today.

Response: **We praise you, O God. May we be faithful to our heritage.**

We give thanks for the glorious tapestry of cultures and worship which we weave together; for the gifts of beauty and of truth we offer to each other; for the sense that our unity in Christ is a harmony of rich diversity in which we all give and receive.

Response: **We praise you, O Christ. May we see your face, and know your grace, in one another.**

We give thanks for the deep conviction that God is not finished with us yet, that in his purpose of unity for his whole creation we are given our place and our mission.

Response: **We praise you, O Holy Spirit. May we have the courage to follow wherever you lead. Amen.**

* * *

111

A PRAYER FOR FAITHFULNESS

> When our hearts are waiting, our spirits expectant, our hopes and fears too vulnerable to express;
> **Christ of the Bethlehem stable, be born in us.**

> When our lives seem good and free, and we feel your wind and your sun on our faces;
> **Christ of the roads of Galilee, walk with us.**

> When the path ahead seems hard and stony, when we see only suffering around and before us, when our hearts cry out for reasons why;
> **Christ of the Gethsemane garden, weep with us.**

> When we feel the powers of darkness have overcome, when the victory of death seems final and desolate;
> **Christ of the cross of Calvary, watch with us.**

> When at last we end our pilgrimage and reach the city of your building, when we commit our poor lives into your care;
> **Christ of the empty tomb, welcome us.**

III. EVANGELISM AND COMMUNICATION

The years 1991-2000 are to be a Decade of Evangelism. Not surprisingly, one of the Sections of ACC-8 was given the special responsibility of discussing evangelism together with communication. Evangelism will not be effective if the good news cannot be communicated.

Discussion centred on the report of the Mission Issues and Strategy Advisory Group (MISAG-2), 'Renew our vision in mission', which was specially written for ACC-8. It builds on the work of earlier meetings of the ACC, the Lambeth Conference 1988, and the reflections of more recent conferences on evangelism.

In its Introduction the report defines strategy as 'the method or means by which we seek to reach our given goals'. It warns, however, that 'the early Church did not begin with a carefully devised mission strategy' and points to the fact that 'in many parts of the world the principal way of sharing the good news of Jesus is by telling stories, both biblical and from contemporary experiences'.

It retells many such stories, and members of the Section echoed them in stories of their own experiences. We set out three below.

The MISAG-2 report also reproduces the full text of the statement made by the Primates of the Anglican Communion and issued after their meeting in Larnaca, Cyprus, in April 1989.

The Section was specially interested in this statement, not only because of the significance of its authorship, but because it offers some elements of a possible strategy for the Decade.

The context of discussion: our stories

I.   One Sunday in a village in Bangladesh a man went to church. He had never been before. Why did he go? He had attended the funeral of a member of the congregation and liked what he had heard said about the person. He knew he wanted to become that kind of a man and have similar things said about him when he died. This is the story of one man's journey into membership of his local church.

II.   John is a priest in the Church of Rwanda, which has an extensive programme of training in evangelism. In his Diocese there are 570 catechists serving 600 churches. Between 10 and 20 churches form a parish. Every three months his catechists attend a week-long training session in evangelism. They are arranged in deaneries or archdeaconries. As a pastor John also attends training twice a year to help him in his leadership of the catechists.

III.   The time is the state of emergency in South Africa, when many were detained. A priest visits a detainee in hospital. He takes a few parishioners with him. The detainee is deeply encouraged by this caring, Christian presence. He begins to find new faith and hope in life.

Some elements of our response

The Section carefully considered many stories, the statement from the Primates, the present situation, the introductory addresses and special papers delivered to the Council, and other documents mentioned in the course of this report. They want to make observations under the five following headings, and pose a number of questions which member Churches, Dioceses and local congregations may like to consider.

CHANGE
The shift from maintenance to mission, as focused in the Decade of Evangelism, will change the Church. Change is evidence of life. Changes are taking place in worship, awareness, communication,

care, witness and proclamation. Men and women are being trans-formed by the Gospel. Mission will bring change to the Church. The communicators too will experience change as they become more open to the audience, less restricted and self-conscious, introducing different emphases as the needs of those around are felt and their response is made.

What changes are taking place in your church?

FAITHFULLY OBEDIENT

There is a four-fold cord always drawing the Church into mission:
  The needs of the local world
  Experienced reality of Christian truths
  The Lord's great commission
  The constraining love of Christ
  (See 2 Cor 5.)

Christians are sent as lambs among wolves, travelling and travailing on the way that is Christ's, going to people in the place they call home, and sharing the good news (Luke 10.1-10).

There is a cost in the way of the cross which the Church is invited to follow. Particular churches grow and diminish, but they are called to be witnesses and to proclaim that 'Jesus Christ is Lord'. Lukewarm discipleship in a church is repudiated by her Lord (Rev 3.16). Increased numbers, while very important, cannot be regarded as the sole measure of the success of evangelism.

Where is obedience to the faith leading in your church?

EXPECTANT HOPE

The Church's dependence on her Lord is often measured by her prayer life, including intercession. Intercession can sometimes be in such general terms that the blessing of the particular answer goes unidentified. The ministry of prayer for the needs of the community and individuals can be of great benefit to the community of faith as well as to those for whom prayer is offered. The Church that expects God to work often sees that happen.

Are there ways of encouraging the worship and prayers of your church?

THE LOCAL CHURCH

'Nothing happens until it happens locally.' It is important that each local church has its own plan for the Decade of Evangelism. At the same time it is wise not to depend only on one strategy. We have noted a list of strategies identified by MISAG-2, including: Base Christian

Communities (small groups of active Christians, formed usually in third world countries in conditions of social deprivation, where previous Christian influence has declined); Marriage Encounter (studies of the issues of marriage within a Christian frame of reference, for couples who are perhaps on the fringe of church life); and the Cursillo Movement (retreats for study and renewal). Strategies have to be those that suit the circumstances, as well as showing the individuals who make up the local congregation that their distinctive characteristics and gifts are fully valued. Shy, retiring people are just as important as those who are more forthcoming.

The culture of the local church must be understood and taken seriously. By culture we mean the church's historic background and its present way of living, as well as the local customs it has taken into its life.

Christ's life on earth should be expressed not only through individual witness and the gathered congregation. There is room for the small group as well as for the larger assembly.

The clergy and laity who make up the leadership team should adopt the style of leadership to mobilise the local church which best corresponds to that church's special needs. An authoritative approach may be appropriate in some cultures, but it is not always so.

When was the life of your local church last reviewed and assessed?

Could local strategies be shared within your Church or Diocese?

To what extent is your church dominated by (a) tradition, or (b) what is of help to the present members, or (c) the culture of the locality?

What steps are being taken to give training in evangelism to those in leadership?

Is your church fully welcoming to strangers and newcomers?

THE COMMUNITY OF THE SPIRIT

A distinctive mark of the Christian Church is love and acceptance of the individual. If pastoral care of one another in the local church is missing, then its witness becomes a denial of the God who is love. Participation in the community of love by every member is crucial. This means showing that all people are valued by the church, including the elderly and the young, and helping each contribute to the life of the whole in appropriate ways.

The community of the Spirit not only shows the love of the Father; it is centred on Christ Jesus, and is open to the life-giving Spirit whose fruit and gifts are known. Anglican tradition speaks of the congregation as being the community where the word of God is preached and the sacraments faithfully administered.

Section reports

There is a distinctiveness about the Christian which should be seen and known. The standards of the Church and the secular world will often be in conflict. However, the Church should not be awkward or unloving towards those apparently outside the Christian faith.

Christian witness is often most effective where people use openings within their own social grouping.

The local church needs plans to use the opportunities for ministry at the times of birth, marriage, death etc.

Change and advance can seem like a threat to worshippers, particularly to those who were born and nurtured in 'their' church. Great compassion and sensitivity has to be shown; sometimes growth can be painful.

Damage may be done to the community of the Spirit by disruptions from both within and outside the local church. Both have potential for spoiling the witness of the community and its ability to communicate effectively.

What areas of care could be strengthened in your local church?

Are there ways in which members can be helped in their daily witness?

Do members of your local church take personal holiness of life seriously?

In what ways are divisions within the Church being worked out for the sake of the unity for which Christ prayed?

What plans does your church have for preparation and follow-up of its pastoral ministry at birth, marriage, death etc?

Some major questions

WHEN THE CHURCH EVANGELISES, WHAT EXPERIENCE ARE WE INVITING PEOPLE TO SHARE?

This would be answered in many ways, by the various traditions that go to make up the life of the Anglican Communion. It might be summarised by saying that it is the Lordship of Jesus Christ and its expression in daily life.

HOW DO PEOPLE COME TO FAITH?

This question can be answered in two ways:

1   Through the secret and sovereign work of the Holy Spirit.
2   Through as many ways as there are people in the Church.

Both answers are equally true, and neither should be overlooked. The first leads the Church to its knees in prayer, while the second asks that all the God-given skills, gifts and wisdom are used creatively in evangelism in the local context.

It is suggested that each church undertakes an inquiry to discover in what ways those who have joined the Church over the last two years came into membership. The answers will show areas where further results could be achieved.

The local church can also learn from:
  (a) the experience of other member Churches or Dioceses or local congregations;
  (b) evangelists who could help in mission and evangelism;
  (c) publications, videos and training schemes;
  (d) other denominations, agencies and Christian communities.

Careful use should be made of evangelistic programmes. To use an analogy from education, the question is not 'How do you teach?' but rather 'How does learning take place?' The local context dictates the programme and the methods.

There must be a dependence on God by the Church, looking for a movement of the Holy Spirit among the people being served, loved and approached in Christ's name.

HOW DO LOCAL PEOPLE KNOW THEMSELVES TO BE VALUED BY THE CHURCH AND BY CHRISTIANS?

The story in Luke 7.36-50, of the woman who anointed Jesus's feet, shows that love overcame the distractions of the situation. She knew herself accepted and forgiven. It was not words but actions that counted. Women and men know themselves to be loved and valued without being told in so many words.

Some church members do not have friends outside their congregations; the life of the church takes up all their time. Changing this situation is the task of the whole congregation, as well as of the individual.

There may be areas of local life where there are needs which are not being met by others. It is right that attempts should be made by the church to meet them.

In some parts of the Communion, society is splintering into communities based on interests rather than on geographical location. Ministry might focus on groups centred on such things as farming, industry, sport or medicine.

After those who have drawn near to the church have begun to worship and actually 'belong', the community needs to show that it continues to care about them and value them.

117

HOW DOES THE CHURCH COMMUNICATE THE GOOD NEWS OF JESUS CHRIST?

Through all that the Church says and all that the Church is: this is an over-simplified way of putting an evident truth.

The apostle Paul indicated that the Church, when it meets for worship, should cause the outsider also to 'worship God and declare that God is really among you' (1 Cor 14.25). The worshipping community communicates as it worships. What is communicated by its symbols, buildings, music, colour, liturgy and much else besides?

The Church also communicates by:

(a) the care it shows to the outsider as well as among its members, through nurture and service;

(b) a lifestyle true to the Gospel and sensitive to the needs of the local situation;

(c) the involvement of its members within the life of the local community, aiming at transforming society;

(d) being in and of the local culture, yet without yielding to compromise that might damage its witness.

'What you are speaks so loudly that I can't hear what you're saying.'

Oral witness, testimony and proclamation remain essential. Evangelism is giving an account of what is seen in the Christian community, so that others may come to share in that same life of the Spirit.

(i) The personal story expressed simply is a powerful form of evangelism. Sharing is usually best done on a one-to-one basis, though the public telling of the personal story has its place. Often this starts by church members telling one another how they came to faith. This gives confidence when an opportunity arises to share the story with someone who is outside the 'household of faith'.

(ii) The evangelistic home meeting works well in some parts of the Communion, while others find that visiting those on the fringe of church life at a time of crisis can present many opportunities for evangelism.

(iii) Drama, music, film or video, and dance can serve as vehicles for evangelism, although the message may need to be presented in a variety of ways when using such art forms.

(iv) The gift of the preacher-evangelist is as much in evidence as ever, and should not be ignored by the local church.

There needs to be encouragement of those who are called to speak and act on behalf of the exploited and alienated.

The thought-forms and understanding of the local culture should never be overlooked. Many factors need to be considered: whether or not there is a local tradition of faith; the attitudes and values shown in radio, television and newspapers; the places and character of social meeting; the educational background of the people etc.

The scandal of the disunity of the Church cannot be ignored, and demands the development of mutual trust with other believers. This is an essential part of our witness.

The Anglican Church is not primarily in the business of communicating Anglicanism, but it must be remembered that the outsider will encounter the good news with an Anglican flavour.

Finally, the Church that does not communicate the life-giving power of Christ is in danger of dying. The Church that takes communication seriously will experience change. May the Lord of the Church give us direction.

The Decade of Evangelism

The following statement about the Decade of Evangelism was made by the Primates of the Anglican Communion, meeting in Larnaca, Cyprus, in April 1989.

> To proclaim the good news of the Kingdom;
> To teach, baptize and nurture new believers;
> To respond to human need by loving service;
> To seek to transform the unjust structures of society.

1 Thus did ACC-6, meeting in Badagry in 1984, summarise the mission of the Church. The Anglican Communion was urged to review its total life in the light of its missionary calling. From this 'mission audit' undertaken in many Dioceses, there began to emerge a renewed emphasis on our evangelistic task. Thus it was that the Lambeth Conference of 1988 called on Provinces and Dioceses of the Anglican Communion, in co-operation with other Christians, to make the closing years of this millennium a Decade of Evangelism (Lambeth Resolution 43).

2 Subsequent to Lambeth, the Mission Issues and Strategy Advisory Group (MISAG-2) made helpful comments and suggestions regarding this proposal, including this definition of evangelism:

> Jesus commanded his disciples to 'go and make disciples of all nations . . . and be my witnesses . . . to the ends of the earth' (Matt 28.19; Acts 1.8). To evangelise is to make known by word and deed the love of the crucified and risen Christ in the power of the

Holy Spirit, so that people will repent, believe and receive Christ as their Saviour and obediently serve him as their Lord in the fellowship of his Church. (See also John 20.21; Luke 4.18f.)

The primacy of evangelism derives not from a desire simply to increase church numbers, but from God's unique provision of eternal life in Jesus Christ.

The Primates wish to commend the attached reflections of MISAG-2 to individual Provinces and Dioceses, as well as those reflections contained in the earlier report of MISAG-1, entitled 'Giving mission its proper place'. The report of the Mission and Ministry section of the Lambeth Conference (especially sections 1-23) is also to be commended. In all these reports our people will find a theological and practical basis for effective strategies of evangelism.

3   The Primates of the Anglican Communion want, therefore, to affirm this call to a Decade of Evangelism, and request all Dioceses, parishes and religious communities to prepare for the Decade with prayer.

We suggest the following guidelines for consideration by the individual Provinces:

(a) *Approach the Decade of Evangelism not as a terminal point but as a beginning.* We carry on the Decade as learners expecting its end to be followed by decade after decade of evangelism. God's calling and sending forth are measured not by decades, but by eternity.

(b) *Discover and use distinctive Anglican gifts.* Our heritage of liturgical and sacramental worship, our apostolic continuity, and our 'reasonable tolerance' are all evangelistic tools and distinctive gifts to the larger Christian community. Effective evangelists are true to themselves.

(c) *Seek to work co-operatively with Christians of other Churches,* many of which are also calling for a Decade of Evangelism. Two significant conferences in 1989—the World Council of Churches sponsored 'Your Will Be Done: Mission in Christ's Way' in San Antonio, and the meeting of 'Lausanne II' in Manila—will indicate numerous ecumenical opportunities for co-operation and sharing at all levels.

(d) *Focus on persons not programmes.* The Christian faith is spread person to person, community to community. It is a movement. It is not a programme passed down for others to follow. Human story touches human story in the midst of God's story.

(e) *Focus on the local not the universal.* The context of evangelism is crucial. Some Anglicans live in a predominantly Christian culture; others are in the minority. Strategies for—even definitions of—evangelism may well vary from situation to situation.

(f) *Learn from each other.* Living in many different situations and contexts, Anglicans have much to learn from each other and from other Christians. Provinces are therefore encouraged to gather statements, stories, strategies and experiences for sharing with other Anglicans and the larger Christian community. The Anglican Consultative Council, through the secondment of a Volunteer for Mission, will seek to co-ordinate and facilitate this sharing, as well as the identification of further resources.

(g) *Use of the laity,* the forefront missionaries of the Church. Tremendous energy is released when we realise that every Christian is an agent of mission.

(h) *Prayer is essential.* Surround and undergird all ministries of evangelism and new initiatives for evangelism with prayer.

4   Meeting so close to the world of our biblical origins, we are reminded that the God who called forth and sent out Abraham and Sarah and the Prophets, who in the fullness of time sent forth his only Son and the Holy Spirit, our Comforter, is the same God who continues to call forth and send out his faithful people on that mission of reconciliation which is God's own. Jesus Christ in his ministry, in his life, death and resurrection, modelled that mission for us. It involves no less than the fullest measure of service and proclamation. In a Decade of Evangelism we seek for a moment to lift up this great act of proclamation, properly called evangelism, which holds out to women and men everywhere the person of Jesus Christ. As people in the power of the Holy Spirit are drawn to him, so are they drawn to God, to one another and to all creation. On this sure foundation may be built all our ministries of love.

COMMENTS ON THE PRIMATES' STATEMENT

It was noted that the four-fold summary of mission propounded at ACC-6, which appears at the head of the Primates' statement, evolved from successive meetings of the ACC and was adopted by the Lambeth Conference 1988. The word 'mission' is used to cover all aspects of the Church's obligation to advance the Kingdom of God. The word 'evangelism' was introduced following the Lambeth Conference Resolutions (particularly 42-44).

It is argued by some that this development has led to a confusion of concepts. Paragraph 2 of the statement clearly indicated the special character of evangelism, which is narrower than the ideas conveyed by 'mission'. Nevertheless the choice of title, Decade of Evangelism, did contribute to a confusion of the concepts of evangelism and mission, not least when the statement looks for an effective Decade in terms of the often quoted four-fold definition of mission.

It has become quite clear during ACC-8 that the introduction of the word 'evangelism' as the definitive title for this Decade has caused anxiety, even apprehension in some Churches of the Communion where explicit evangelism for the Christian faith is suspect or even illegal. The Section therefore hopes that discretion will be exercised where appropriate over the use of the title commended by the Primates.

The Section was also aware of a subtle difference of title given to the Decade by different Christian groups, some calling it a Decade of Evangelism, others a Decade of Evangelisation. This is not simply a difference of use between Anglicans and Roman Catholics. Already one Diocese of the Church of England has elected to speak of a Decade of Evangelisation.

We sincerely hope that subtle differences in nomenclature will not distract Christians from their main obligation to advance the Kingdom, nor inhibit close co-operation between all Christians on whom the same obligation rests.

We have to note, however, that the call of the Lambeth Conference for co-operation with other Christians to make the closing years of the millennium a Decade of Evangelism has fallen on deaf ears in many Churches of the Anglican Communion. We urge that greater publicity should be given to the reports of both the Lausanne II conference and the WCC San Antonio conference.

Further discussion of the Decade revealed that for some there was an impression that the object was to 'do good' rather than preach the message of Christ crucified.

With regard to the Primates' hope that full preparation be made for the Decade, the Section is anxious that it should be placed on record that more than 400 religious communities were already offering daily prayer and intercessions for the work ahead.

Observing that the Primates saw this Decade not as a terminal point but as the first of successive Decades, the Section acknowledged the definite advantages in ten-year 'exercises' as affording regular opportunities for evaluation of work done in the previous ten years, in the light of which further, perhaps more effective, work could be undertaken. It is not to be assumed that all work will be equally successful or appropriate for repetition in later years.

As regards the matter of 'discovering and using Anglican gifts', some members of the Section had difficulty in identifying such gifts. Others emphasised that for them and in their cultures, one of the distinctions of the Anglican Church was that its members, many of them young people, were active in sharing their faith.

It became clear that cultural background and experience fundamentally influenced the ways and means by which the Communion could undertake mission in its various member Churches. In South India, for example, the Mothers' Union had acted on the WCC document offering food and assistance to the needs of local communities. The result had been a kindling of interest in Christian values and motivation, and a number of converts to Christianity.

The Section was especially attracted to the Primates' insistence on the person-to-person nature of the work of the Decade. Precisely because of this, we appreciated the sensitivity needed to ensure that evangelism was effective, indeed in some communities even acceptable.

In this regard, the need to learn from each other's successes and failures seemed self-evident. For some, the consecration of 'missionary' bishops might seem appropriate; for others, the task might be better placed in the hands of enablers, clerical or lay. Church 'planting' is successful in some member Churches, but not necessarily appropriate for all.

If lay members are to be engaged in this work of the Decade, then it is apparent that there is a world-wide need to ensure that the Church knows how to engage their skills and enthusiasms. In the Sudan and in Nigeria, practical measures have been taken to ensure that clergy and laity are trained together. In Chile, 80 per cent of all training for mission is taken up by lay people.

The point was made, however, that all laity are sent out as part of the Church's mission even if they are not specifically qualified as 'lay assistants' by virtue of training.

Above all, the Section wishes to underline the emphasis in the Primates' statement of the absolute *necessity,* not just the general desirability, of the Decade being carried out by the member Churches, their Dioceses and parishes. 'World culture' is a figment of the imagination of popularists. Local cultures, reflecting the developments of local history, are the real world in which we live, in and to which the Gospel is proclaimed and can be proclaimed effectively.

Section reports

LANGUAGE

On any interpretation, communication must involve language. So far, failure to ensure the translation of relevant documents for the Decade into and from English, Spanish, French and Swahili and perhaps other languages is to be regretted. Volunteer translators need to be actively recruited. Isolation and serious misunderstanding may be the result of neglect in this field.

OTHER WORLD FAITHS

The Church is constantly faced with the claims made by other living faiths, particularly Islam, Buddhism, Hinduism etc. Evangelism in this context means undertaking dialogue with the other faiths, which can be a costly process. This dialogue may require a change within Christians as well, not in terms of their relationship with Christ, but in their understanding of dogma, tradition, and Church paraphernalia which may be confused by them with the truths of the faith.

THE NEW AGE

The scientific age of the enlightenment has robbed secular humanity of a sense of mystery and meaning. This has resulted in a despairing search by many for experiences that bring feelings of wellbeing and fulfilment. The real possibility of the annihilation of the planet Earth and the universe by the misuse of nuclear power, the pollution of the atmosphere, and the rapid demise of plant and animal species has led some to believe in a coming Age of Aquarius. Keeping in touch with a life force is seen to be an essential preparation for this 'New Age'. The beliefs propagated tend to be a broad assortment of eastern religions, disciplines and miscellaneous practices, all seeking to bring comfort and enlightenment through the individual self.

Evangelism is the communicating of the good news of Jesus Christ. It means entering into a relationship with the person of Christ. It means acknowledging our need for him: for his healing and forgiveness, experiencing and accepting that we depend totally on him. For this reason evangelism contrasts sharply with, and is a challenge to, what might be called the 'New Age' culture. By this we mean the one-sided concentration of concern on the individual and his or her own inner potential for life and growth. Evangelism means communicating the message that we need the Lord and that he is the source of life and growth.

ADVISER FOR THE DECADE OF EVANGELISM

We are encouraged to note the appointment for two years of the Revd

Canon Robert Renouf as Adviser for the Decade of Evangelism.

Canon Renouf is responsible to the Secretary General of the ACC for promoting and co-ordinating the sharing of the distinctive contributions of the member Churches in terms of stories, strategies and experiences and for further resources for evangelism. His duties have included, but are not necessarily limited to, serving as an enabler, resource person, liaison to the member Churches, communicator, and theologian.

Under the direction of Canon Renouf, ACC is planning ahead to 1991, when support for launching and carrying out the Decade will be required. A follow-up report will be made to the Primates at their meeting in Ireland in April 1991.

ACC SUPPORT FOR THE DECADE

The ACC has been helping the member Churches get ready for the Decade of Evangelism, in the first place by appointing an Adviser.

Prayer, what Henri Nouwen has called 'the language of the Christian community', is central. The religious communities, along with member Churches, Dioceses, parishes, congregations and institutions, are engaged in prayer for the Decade. They have been aided by the use of prayer cards produced by the ACC, containing original prayers from member Churches throughout the Communion. To date over 7,000 copies of each of two prayer cards have been distributed to Primates, provincial secretaries, religious communities, theological seminaries and training colleges, mission agencies, news services and all those receiving *Anglican information,* which includes all the bishops of the Communion.

ACC support has been carried forward in (i) planning (exploring, with the Primates, ways of proceeding and possible designs), (ii) preparation (helping the member Churches establish the conditions in which the Decade can be implemented effectively), and (iii) promoting (assisting in turning vision and planning into practice and actual proclamation).

SHARING

These three steps call for inspiration and animation, giving life to the Church and Christians through the sharing of stories, strategies, statements and experiences from different parts of the Communion. Sharing is being encouraged by ACC through prayer cards, a newsletter entitled *Sharings,* a book that will help Churches move from vision to practice (funded by the Church Mission Publishing Company) and a video (under the direction of the Revd Dr Robert T.

Browne) showing mission and evangelism taking place in various Churches of the Communion throughout the world.

Speaking engagements, consultations, personal contacts and correspondence with members of member Churches are also means of sharing carried on regularly as part of the process of making preparations for the Decade.

LAUNCHING

The next phase after planning and preparation will be the launching of the Decade by the member Churches. Each member Church will launch separately rather than there being one global launching.

PROCLAMATION

The Decade will involve public proclamation, declaring and announcing openly the good news as an essential part of mission, engaging the Churches of the world. The style of such proclamation must be appropriate to the local church and circumstances.

SHIFT TO MISSION

The Decade will challenge the Churches of the Communion to bring about a shift from maintenance to mission. Such a shift will require radical change in structures in parishes, Dioceses and member Churches. Effective training of laity and clergy for mission and evangelism (especially cross-cultural) will be imperative. This, in many instances, will require training that will enable every baptized person to become an agent of transformation and change for the building of the Kingdom. The difficulty of motivating those who form the present Church needs to be addressed, so that the desire to share their faith in appropriate ways leads to action.

MISSIOLOGY—ECUMENICAL CONVERGENCE

It has often been pointed out that, as Christians reflect on mission and evangelism, there has recently been a remarkable convergence within the statements produced: Roman Catholic and Anglican, ecumenical and evangelical. Within these the theology of mission is shown to be basic, traditional, biblical, and yet in many ways radical.

Mission is central to the life of the Church on earth, as it engages with the cultural context of the world in which it is called to witness through nurture, loving service and transformation, as well as proclamation. Such convergence is welcomed, as is the recent Common Declaration by the Pope and the Archbishop of Canterbury. Further work is called for, particularly at the more local level.

Conclusion

It is of vital importance that all members of ACC-8—primates, bishops, priests and laity—should give high priority to reviewing the preparation for and organisation of the Decade of Evangelism in the individual member Churches they represent. There has been sufficient talk about evangelism. Now is the time to revitalise our mission and embark on the Decade itself.

An equally high priority needs to be given to ways and means of encouraging and monitoring work undertaken during this and later decades. If the Decade is not to be seen as 'terminal', steps should be taken from the outset to consider how it can be kept alive.

REFERENCES
1 The Report of the Mission Issues and Strategy Advisory Group (MISAG-1), 'Giving mission its proper place' (1984)
2 The Report of the Mission and Ministry Section of the Lambeth Conference 1988, *The truth shall make you free,* pp 27-77
3 The Report of MISAG-2, 'Renew our vision in mission' (1990)

IV. UNITY AND CREATION

The earth is the Lord's: a letter to our children

Dear young friends,
                    Have you ever had a letter from someone in Brazil, or India, or New Zealand? This letter is from people in those countries and 37 others as well.

Have you ever shared a letter with someone in Kenya or England or Canada? This letter is going to children in those countries and all around the world.

We want to talk with you about our worries and our hopes about this earth which we all share together. We are a group of Christians from Anglican Churches around the world. We've been meeting in a large house in Wales for the past week. The sun has been shining and it has been very hot. But this morning it is raining softly and this is welcome.

We know that for many of you the rain is not always a friend. Rain can become an enemy when the floods rise. For many others of you the sunshine can become an enemy rather than a friend. For all of you the fact that the world is getting warmer—the 'greenhouse effect'—is a threat to your future.

If only we could talk face to face we would prefer to start by finding out what you think. For example, what do you find beautiful about the world? What worries you about the world? But since we cannot speak to you personally we have remembered stories of young people that we know. By telling these stories we hope that the young people will be able to speak to us and to you, and that we can talk together that way.

We know, and it makes us sad, that some of you have only been able to see the beauty of creation very rarely or very dimly. We know that some of you have been terribly damaged by natural disasters, such as the earthquakes in Iran and the Philippines just a short while ago.

Sometimes we have to recognise that ugliness, disaster and pain are simply part of nature. For example, volcanoes do erupt and earthquakes do happen, and they have helped to make our world the way it is. When people are affected by them it is a tragedy, but nobody is to blame. But there are times when people are responsible for damage to the world, when beaches are covered with oil and filth, forests are cut down, and garbage is rotting in the sun.

Adamu lives in northern Nigeria. When he was a young child he used to wander in the forest behind his village. Then the people of the village began to cut down the trees for logs for buildings and for firewood. But they didn't plant new trees to replace the ones they were cutting down. After ten years the whole village had to move, over 30 miles away, because the desert just moved in and swallowed up the village. Then the people started cutting down the trees in the forest round their new home . . . and within a short while Adamu and his people had to move again as the desert swallowed up their new village.

But in Mali the people used to cook their food in stone cookstoves. They used three large stones with gaps between them for air. The stoves worked well, but they burned wood very quickly, so that a lot of wood was needed to cook a meal. Someone figured out that you could make a better stove with five smaller stones. The small stones would leave smaller gaps, so less air would get in—and you wouldn't have to use so much wood. As a result the people are now using only six pieces of wood for every ten they used before. They are hopeful that now, perhaps, their old trees may last until new ones are ready.

We have to admit that the world we are passing on to you is less than the gift that God intended. This could have been avoided. Beautiful things have often been replaced with ugliness. We want to say we are sorry. Though the world was already in a mess when our parents handed it over to us, we still want to say to you that we are sad we have made it worse. Each of us, in one way or another, has contributed to the mess, and together we share the blame.

Gillian, a teenager in Sydney, Australia, is a keen surfboard rider. When her parents were young, they enjoyed the famous Australian beaches. But Gillian is no longer free to share in such pleasures. Sydney's rubbish and waste, including sewage, has so poisoned the sea that swimming is sometimes dangerous. Also, the atmosphere has become polluted, so that the very air she breathes may be unhealthy. Damage to the ozone layer at higher levels has made it sometimes dangerous to take part in outdoor sport. Gillian has an ambition to help improve things by joining her friends in local and national programmes to fight pollution. Gillian has a vision: that her children will be able to enjoy the world around, just as her parents could.

Christopher, who is nine, lives in Burlington, Ontario. One of the problems in Canada is the amount of rubbish that people make. The children in Christopher's class each bring sandwiches to school, something to drink, perhaps something sweet, and each of these is wrapped. All the wrapping makes a big pile of rubbish every day. Some teachers decided to invent a lunch kit that wouldn't make any rubbish. They designed some containers for sandwiches and drinks that you can take home and wash for the next day, instead of just throwing them out. Christopher thinks this is a good idea. He thinks that when you know there's a problem, you should try to do something about it.

Mind you, our generation has also done its bit to put things right, to try to restore the beauty, and to ensure that the riches of creation are shared out more fairly. Because we know that this is God's world, and because time and again we have discovered that we are working alongside him, we know that it would be wrong to despair. We can go on hoping—and working—even when all seems totally hopeless. The new freedom that people in different countries around the world are beginning to enjoy is proof that the most unlikely things can and do happen.

Bishop Dinis Sengulane tells us that children in Mozambique are going to bring their war toys to the services in church on Sunday 2 September, so that all toy guns can be destroyed in a special ceremony. Even those who have no toys like this are encouraged to buy them, and explain to those who sell them that the purpose of buying them is to destroy them, because the children are friends of the Prince of Peace.

They will explain that in their country many hundreds of thousands of lives have been destroyed by people who just happen to have a gun. They are trying to show that to handle a gun is not something normal, like handling a ball or a cooking pot.

'I have my toy gun just for fun,' said one child when hearing about the message of Peace. 'Your right to fun ends where it threatens my right to be alive,' was the reply.

A great painting allows us to discover the mind and the heart and the skill of the artist. So it is with this world. As we discover its beauty and its richness, so we discover the glory and the wonder of God. At times we want to break into song at the glorious joy of the world around us; there are also times of breathless wonder; and there are times of happy laughter.

The story in Genesis tells us that when God had finished his great work of creation he looked around at it all and saw that it was very good. He enjoyed his creation and loved it very much. When we laugh, when we are silent and when we sing we are sharing in God's joy.

In the island of Mauritius in the Indian Ocean there was once a beautiful bird known as the dodo, which lived happily in the island and multiplied. In the seventeenth century Dutch sailors on their way to the Far East hunted the dodo because they enjoyed eating it after weeks at sea. As a result they wiped it out completely. Today the children of Mauritius can no longer enjoy the beauty of this bird. And creation has lost one of the gifts of God. (Hence the expression 'as dead as the dodo'.)

Archbishop Michael Ramsey, who used to be Archbishop of Canterbury, said that when we meet God, the most important question he will ask is, 'Did you enjoy the world I made for you?'

We want you to enjoy the world which God has created for you. We want to join you in caring for God's world. You will then be able to pass it on to your children. In their turn they will be able to enjoy the gift which God has created for them.

With all our love,

† ROBERT CANTUAR.

POSTSCRIPT TO THE CHURCHES

Here are some practical points we wish to add to what we have written in our letter.

Use the letter The letter is being sent out to the children through the Churches of our Communion. We hope that you will use the letter in any and every way that seems suitable. You may wish simply to add some illustrations, copy it and pass it to children, or take extracts from it, or use it as a model for a letter of your own to suit your own culture and circumstances. What is important is that the conversation with the children begins.

Paint the world We hope that children will be encouraged to react to the letter and so to keep the conversation going. One possible response would be for children to paint pictures of the world as they see and experience it. These pictures, and essays and letters if the response takes those forms, could be shared with companion Dioceses, and might also be taken to such gatherings as the Anglican Encounter in Brazil in 1992 and the Youth Conference in Vancouver in 1993. Or how about chain letters, parishes to parishes or Dioceses to Dioceses?

Curriculum adjustment We hope that those responsible for the nurturing of children in the faith will look to see that the curriculum includes the perception that creation is the gift of God, which we are to enjoy and to care for on behalf of those to whom we shall pass it on.

The sixth of August The story of the destruction of war toys in Mozambique on 2 September is an example which we hope will be followed widely. We are reminded, however, that 6 August, the Feast of the Transfiguration, is already widely taken up as a day to remember the bombing of Hiroshima. To make this observance part of our regular life will enable us to widen our understanding that our concern, and our enjoyment, is to embrace the totality of creation.

Rogationtide In many places the observance of Rogationtide has fallen into disuse. We hope that Churches will encourage imaginative use of this season, focusing on our responsibility for the environment.

Ecumenical and inter-faith activity Our concern for creation is not exclusive to Anglicans. It is our experience that Christians grow together as they work together in a common cause. We hope that Christians of different traditions and members of other faiths will find a variety of ways to work together in caring for and celebrating and enjoying creation.

Government We have given encouragement that our care for God's world should be expressed by our children at the most local level. We hope that Churches will also search out opportunities to express their concern to government and, perhaps by way of joint seminars, to explore possibilities for action at national and global levels.

Unity and creation

Progress towards Christian unity must be set in the context of the wider movement towards the summing up of all things in Christ. One cannot be pursued in isolation from the other, for 'the earth is the Lord's, and everything that is in it'. This has produced a distinct shift in emphasis in recent years. Ecumenical activity is no longer confined to a search for structural unity between the Churches. It now embraces joint involvement in matters of common concern to seek for racial and social harmony and the preservation of the environment. The goals of this wider agenda cannot be attained without pain and struggle, and the journey is long.

As we relate our experiences to each other we see the reality of advances already made and victories already won. Our hopes are not based upon naive sentimentality, but upon God's call to his Church to be one. Within this context even our negative experiences can be regarded as challenges to pursue our aims, and not as final defeat. The light of resurrection shines out of the darkness of death.

Throughout the world, Anglicans come from widely differing cultural and ethnic backgrounds. From this we learn something of the variety of motives which promote our ecumenical endeavour. In some places it will be the needs of education, in others the search for peace, and in others it will be social issues facing the community.

We can also prompt each other to explore new ways of working together: joint worship, social and environmental action, participation in Church meetings and synods, shared pastoral and evangelistic ministries in remote areas, joint eucharistic liturgies and educational projects, the formation of communities to combat deep social, political and religious divisions. It is easy to forget that few of these would have been contemplated only a generation ago.

Nevertheless there remain many challenges and questions that require careful thought. There is frustration that with the shift to a wider agenda there has been a 'cooling off' in relationships at the level of authority and structure which often affects the local scene. In some parts of the world, there is the power of political and ideological systems which exploit denominational differences for their own ends. Local engagement in ecumenism in some places may not be supported by those who hold office at diocesan and national level. There is the gap between the life of the local church and the international dialogue.

There is the need to distinguish between deeper commitment to Christ in and through our respective denominations, and mere 'defensive denominationalism', where membership of a denomination is more important than membership in Christ. Denominational differences are exacerbated by the revival of fundamentalisms and fears. These divisive forces challenge us to pursue reconciliation with a much greater sense of urgency.

Rigorous thought needs to be given to improving opportunities for ecumenical formation for children, lay adults and clergy in religious and theological education.

While all barriers to full communion have not yet fallen, we can be encouraged, for example, by pioneering steps in Anglican–Lutheran relationships in North America and parts of Africa and Europe. We shall make greater advances along that road by discerning together the practical consequences of the mutual recognition of baptism that already exists.

THE LOCAL SCENE

Where Christians of different denominations go out and work together in mission, proclaiming God's rule over all life, they share in God's action in reconciling and transforming the world. Evangelism is one vital part of mission, which includes serving those in need, prophesying against injustice and oppression, and witnessing by lives of love and prayer. If we are to evangelise in this context, we must be sensitive to people's questions and take into consideration the variety of ways in which God works. We should long for people to become members of the Christian community, but we have to overcome denominational partisanship. Mission, including evangelism, demands ecumenical co-operation. Therefore the Decade of Evangelism should be understood in the manner we have described, and engaged in ecumenically (see Lambeth 1988 Resolution 43).

Ecumenical understanding and convergence grow when local churches are able to identify and engage in projects which are important, urgent, and within the capability of the community. Although co-operation should take place at all levels, it is at the local parish level that there is the greatest possibility of achieving lasting results. Such activity needs the encouragement of Church leaders and the use of appropriate resources. The media are important here. Parish churches have the opportunity to attract the attention of local press, radio and television, both to produce original Christian material and to participate in secular programmes.

Anglican parishes, in preparing for their work in evangelism, will benefit from programmes which welcome and involve other churches in planning and activity. Co-operation in the coming Decade will be a significant advance towards greater unity among Christians.

NATIONAL COUNCILS OF CHURCHES

Councils of Churches are a primary form of ecumenical co-operation. The work of national councils of Churches is complemented by regional (e.g. All-African, European) councils and by the World Council of Churches (WCC).

In many places councils of Churches have been able to carry out tasks which member Churches have been unable to do by themselves. We must constantly guard against councils becoming para-Churches or another layer of bureaucracy. In order to overcome that, it is important that member Churches provide adequate opportunity for their representatives to report back, so that the member Church can 'own' the work of the council.

In many parts of the world, restructuring of the existing councils of Churches is taking place. This process is seen, not simply as a means of achieving more effective co-operation, but as a step in the pilgrimage towards closer Christian unity. Therefore, the significant increase in the number of councils in which the Roman Catholic Church is involved is a source of joy.

We hope that new structures will lead to greater involvement of member Church decision-makers, to an openness to accepting new membership and to truly united concern and action.

In some places it is being recognised that work done by one member Church need not be duplicated, but can be accepted by all. For example in Canada, when Churches developed a campaign for the abolition of the death penalty, it was agreed that the United Church of Canada should do the necessary research and lead the campaign, while other member Churches of the council gave their support and agreement at the crucial points of the process. This pattern of co-operation can be used at all levels.

THE WORLD COUNCIL OF CHURCHES

We affirm our continued commitment and express our gratitude to the WCC, whose work particularly in the area of relief has been a vital witness. Equally, the work of the Faith and Order Commission has contributed immensely to mutual Christian understanding (e.g. *Baptism, eucharist and ministry*).

The Roman Catholic Church participates as a full member of the Faith and Order Commission, and is involved with the WCC in other ways. We hope that, as with some national councils of Churches, structured ways can be found to enable Roman Catholic membership in the World Council itself, so that the WCC may be more truly representative of God's universal Church.

In the past, Anglican involvement has depended upon contributions from individual Churches, and there is room for the Anglican Communion as a whole to make a greater impact by acting in concert for the benefit of the Communion and the Council.

We therefore suggest that:

(a) Those representing Anglican member Churches of the WCC, as delegates to Canberra, as Committee members or as Anglicans on the WCC staff, meet together immediately before the Canberra assembly to plan their contribution.

(b) A network should be formed of those involved in the WCC on behalf of the Anglican member Churches.

(c) Churches should be encouraged to ensure that delegates are able to report to their national bodies as soon as possible after Canberra.

Another way for Anglicans to contribute more positively to the thinking and operation of the WCC is to ensure that there are more Anglicans on the WCC staff. We affirm the value of the contribution of past and present Anglican staff (the numbers of which do not fully reflect the strength of the Anglican Communion), and we ask Provincial Secretaries to take steps to circulate notices of WCC staff vacancies as widely as possible. We ask member Churches to view such work as important, and to consider seconding staff. We need also to keep in touch with Anglicans working for the WCC in Geneva, and to ease the path of re-entry for them when their contract ends.

INTER-CHURCH RELATIONS

This Council has taken note of the ecumenical resolutions of the Lambeth Conference 1988, Resolutions 3-8. We welcome the practice of interim eucharistic fellowship between Anglicans and Lutherans in North America and between the Church of England and the Evangelical Churches in both Germanys. We are also aware of less formal but nonetheless real instances of communion between Anglicans and Lutherans in parts of Africa. We affirm efforts in these and other places towards full communion and recommend that channels be opened so that they may encourage each other in ways appropriate to their various historical and cultural contexts. Differing historical arrangements between Anglicans and the Nordic and Baltic Churches should also be regularised and play their role in the growing convergence. Christians in their local situations should be encouraged to study *The Niagara report: Report of the Anglican–Lutheran Consultation on Episcope 1987* (1988), and to state whether in their view this could properly lead to full reconciliation between the two communions.

It is good that conversations between Anglicans and the Eastern Orthodox Churches continue, and that relationships with the Oriental Orthodox also go forward. In the latter instance we regret that the next meeting of the Forum is not scheduled before 1993. We hope that its report may be available to the next meeting of the ACC. In the same way we support the idea that local Churches should respond to the report on Anglican–Reformed Church relations entitled *God's reign and our unity,* and hope that the small continuation committee will be able to work out appropriate models of dialogue.

With regard to the ARCIC Final Report, we urge Churches to make their response known to the ACC if they have not already done so. It

An ecumenical gathering. The Archbishop of Canterbury with, left to right, Canon Stephen Platten (his Secretary for Ecumenical Affairs), Bishop Sigisbert Kraft (Old Catholic Church), Dr Eugene Brand (Lutheran Church), Bishop Philipose Mar Chrysostom (Mar Thoma Church), Monsignor Kevin McDonald (Roman Catholic Church), Dr Henry Wilson (Reformed Churches) and Dr Donald Anderson (ACC Ecumenical Officer).

seems to us now that the subject of universal primacy should be examined by ARCIC II within the context of primacy, collegiality and conciliarity. There are wide-ranging and varying perceptions of this issue throughout the Communion.

We note that not all Churches have responded to the report on *Baptism, eucharist and ministry* (BEM) and recommend that those who have not done so should be strongly urged to do so. We should see that the Report is translated into appropriate languages, that the amount of explanatory material is well publicised and that Churches should be encouraged to study the text 'Confessing one faith'.

The preceding notes on international dialogues have reference to Lambeth Resolutions 3-8. We also wish to affirm in substance the Lambeth Resolutions 9-12 and hope that they may be implemented in appropriate ways.

Finally, we ask for a theological study of the experience of the United Churches in full communion (Lambeth Resolution 12), in Bangladesh, North India, Pakistan and South India, to learn from that experience of moving into communion with other Christians. We also suggest that there should be a study, with the United Churches and the WCC, of the terms 'full communion' and 'inter-communion' in ecumenical documents including the Bonn Agreement.

We recognise that theological education is an important part of the Church's mission. Information is needed from every part of the Anglican Communion, and Churches should be asked to send in to the ACC full details of what is happening in their areas regarding the Christian formation of people.

INTER-FAITH RELATIONS

Lambeth Conference Resolutions 20 and 21 dealt with issues of inter-faith dialogue. Since then, the Ecumenical Advisory Group of ACC has met in Mauritius, and has noted the importance of the 'new ecumenism': that is, the intersection of the world's living religions. We recognise that there is a special historical relationship between Christianity and Judaism, and we urge those Christians and Jews who are in dialogue to give careful attention to the issues of justice and peace that affect life in what is the Holy Land for Judaism, Christianity and Islam.

Inter-faith dialogue and mission are two sides of the same coin. There are many instances throughout the world of inter-faith conflict and unhealthy tension, and these are frequently, perhaps usually, related to practical matters, for example the provision of distinctive schools for Muslim children and the provision of Sharî'a courts. Great sensitivity is needed when considering matters of inter-faith worship. A case in point is the use and possible purchase of Christian churches by non-Christian faiths. This is especially true in the case of Islam, which has a great many large communities in the western world. We note with regret that much triumphalist publicity is given out whenever Christian churches are handed over in whatever way to Muslim assemblies. Dialogue between different faiths must begin from the standpoint of integrity, honesty and truth on all sides. Harmony is threatened or made impossible in the face of the growing aggressiveness that is evidenced in some religions. The increase of militant fundamentalism in the three monotheistic religions is at best unhelpful and at worst life-threatening. We commend to the international Christian community the importance of fellowship, friendship and dialogue with people of other faiths.

THE ANGLICAN CENTRE IN ROME

The Anglican Centre in Rome was born 25 years ago. Those who conceived it had a vision of an Anglican presence in Rome which would further Anglican–Roman Catholic unity by nurturing personal relationships and dialogue through changing times, personalities and issues. Anglicans from every Church of the Communion have used the resources of the Centre and benefited from the friendly working relationships established by successive directors of the Centre with colleagues in the Roman Curia.

In every institution, vision of what could be possible must be renewed if it is to continue to be faithful to the original purpose, and serve those for whom it exists with energy and imagination. We are at a particularly good time in our life together to consider the character and style of the Centre. Our ecumenical dialogues and relationships have matured, and ecumenical action and life blooms creatively in many local places; there is a greater confidence and stability. We are deeply concerned about our own family life and those bonds of affection that bind us together. This is particularly so as we discover increasing variety in the expression of our faithfulness to the Gospel, our priorities and our needs. We face heavy demands on our limited financial resources. All of these make consideration of the role and style of the Centre both opportune and essential. We look for a Centre in Rome which will effectively present the ethos of the Anglican Communion in all its variety, its beauty and its ferment. We seek to develop a dialogue in which Anglicans are invited not only to learn something of the Roman Catholic Church and the Vatican, but encouraged to speak with honesty and integrity about the common ground which we share with Roman Catholics, as well as exploring those areas where our traditions diverge.

These concerns have received considerable attention. A special committee, appointed by the Primates when they met in Cyprus in 1989, to consider the Centre's role, style and financing, produced a report with recommendations.

The Primates' Standing Committee, after considering the report, recommended that the Centre should continue for the immediate future in its present location with a Governing Body which can be easily convened and is able to exercise close oversight.

We have had the benefit of oral submissions from the Right Revd E.G. Luscombe, Chairperson of both the Inter-Anglican Finance Committee and of the Primates' Special Committee on the Anglican Centre in Rome, and from the Director of the Centre, the Revd Canon Howard Root. We accept the Primates' recommendations as outlined in the resolution on the Centre. (See Resolution 18, pp161-162).

The Centre has an almost autonomous life, with a Constitution and Council of its own, and looks to the ACC for financial support. Since constitutional amendment is undertaken by the Council of the Anglican Centre in Rome, and requires only the ratification of the amendment by an ordinary vote at a meeting of the ACC, we recommend that:

1. The ACC propose the new Governing Body as an amendment of the Constitution to the Council of the Anglican Centre in Rome, for consideration and adoption at the November meeting of the Council of the Centre, and that the ACC agrees to the necessary ratification.

2. The ACC agrees to make budgetary provision for the next three years, subject to the adoption of amendments to the Centre's constitution, for maximum allocation of £40,000 for each of 1991 and 1992, and £42,250 for 1993, on the understanding that the Governing Body will be completely responsible for funding as soon as possible within the three-year period and no later than the end of 1993.

Unity and healing

We very much hope that what we have written will be a spur to local effort. Making friends with other Christians, moving toward real unity with them and working for the healing of creation is often hard work; but these are Christian imperatives in obedience to, and love of, the Lord of all.

IDENTITY AND AUTHORITY IN THE ANGLICAN COMMUNION

Background and documents studied

ACC-7 recommended that the document 'Unity in diversity in the Anglican Communion: A way forward' be submitted to the Lambeth Conference together with the collated responses to the document from member Churches, and that 'subsequent to the Lambeth Conference the Archbishop of Canterbury in consultation with the Secretary General be requested to appoint a small working group to prepare a report for consideration by ACC-8'. (See *Many gifts one Spirit* p 134.)

The Lambeth Conference adopted two resolutions relevant to the matter of ACC and the Primates' Meeting:

Resolution 18 The Anglican Communion: Identity and Authority;
Resolution 52 Primates' Meeting and ACC.

Subsequently the Standing Committee of ACC prepared a document with the title 'The Anglican Communion: Identity and authority' which, with the concurrence of the Primates' Meeting in Cyprus, 1989, and with responses from some member Churches to which it was circulated, was presented to ACC-8.

At the request of the Secretary General, a paper had been prepared by the Revd David Chaplin on 'Provincial constitutions: Autonomy and interdependence' as a contribution to emerging thought about the nature of the Anglican Communion.

A meeting of representatives from each of the four Sections of ACC-8 was convened to review the discussions that had taken place in the Sections on these two papers, the responses to the former, and a series of questions upon it formulated for the use of the Sections at the suggestion of the Standing Committee.

The group identified a number of issues raised by these documents.

Theological work

A need was felt for more work to be done on the underlying theology of the documents. The proposition that 'the one authority for Anglicans is God' might provide a point of departure. Questions about the nature of the Anglican Communion and its place in the universal Church should be addressed, and the arguments for dispersed or, alternatively, gathered authority should be examined.

The group questioned whether this work should be referred to the proposed Doctrinal Commission, or alternatively whether it could be done by existing Doctrinal Commissions within member Churches. It might on the other hand have to be referred to both. (See Resolution 21 on pp 162-163.)

Language

Some of the words used in the documents are thought to send the wrong signals. For example, 'authority' itself suggests 'from the top down', papal rather than consultative in style. Should we not be talking about 'communion' throughout rather than 'unity'?

Existing bodies

The group could find no full answers to the questions of what the existing instruments of unity were there to do, who co-ordinates them, who allocates resources between them, and who sets their respective priorities. It was noted that these bodies have undergone a process of evolution in developing their present roles, and that this process was continuing. The group saw no reason why these roles should be set in stone at this moment. Perhaps the Communion should go back to a zero position and ask what are its real needs from such bodies.

The cost of maintaining these structures should be examined, and the question should be raised as to whether this represents the most effective use of the money involved. It may be that a price is being paid for duplication of effort and overlapping consultation.

PRIMATES' MEETING

If anyone can 'represent' the Provinces, the Primates are probably the only people who can. However, there was a nervousness in the group about their exercising any juridical authority as proposed. We thought that the Primates should consult in their Provinces before the Primates' Meetings, to identify the issues to be discussed. Further consultation should take place in the Provinces after the meetings in order to consider implementing the results of the consultative work. The Primates should not become a decision-making body, although clearly their moral authority is generally recognised. The usefulness of the Primates' Meeting was acknowledged, but it was felt that it should be more closely associated with ACC. We do not see this as 'collegiality at its best', as one document suggests.

Section reports

ACC

This may not have the ideal composition at the present time, but it should continue, to provide opportunity for consultation with 'other clergy' and lay people. The group wondered whether it could be reconstituted to include three from each member Church, i.e. bishop (Primate), clergy-person and lay-person, though the financial implications of such a reconstitution were recognised.

The group considered a number of complaints about the present arrangements for ACC meetings. There is a need for a clear procedure in agenda-setting. We received quantities of material not asked for, but no agenda. We flounder in a sea of topics. The agenda should contain at least specific items referred from the ACC itself, from the Lambeth Conference, and from the Standing Committee, with an indication of their respective status.

We need to be aware in more detail of the relationship between the ACC and the Secretariat, and between the ACC Secretariat and Lambeth Palace. It was felt that the Secretariat was in danger of not knowing what 'hat' it was wearing at any given time.

One Section went further, to spell these considerations out in detail as follows:

> The issue which can be tackled more immediately is that of the agenda of ACC. We believe that there should be clear account-ability of the Secretariat to ACC and that there should be at each meeting a clear and precise agenda identifying: all items referred to ACC by any other body; the stage of discussion reached; the decisions needed; and the nature of action required to be taken. At present these turn up almost by accident from the mass of papers. We believe a different form of agenda would identify things referred to us for advice, decision or action, but would not rule out more general discussion on important topics. Such an agenda might be provided from a number of sources, e.g.:
>
> —items directly referred by member Churches;
>
> —items from previous meetings followed up by staff;
>
> —items referred from Lambeth Conferences, Primates' Meetings etc;
>
> —items referred directly from MISAG, the Peace and Justice Network, the International Liturgical Consultation and the Inter-Anglican Theological and Doctrinal Commission.

ARCHBISHOP OF CANTERBURY

It was noted that there was no common view of the place of the Archbishop of Canterbury in provincial constitutions and documents.

Common Declaration

There was no high level of enthusiasm in any Section for the Common Declaration. (See Resolution 21.)

The time factor

A need for urgency had been expressed in the papers referred to above. The view of the group was that the issues must be 'moved along', but given sufficient time and not unduly rushed at the expense of proper consideration at the appropriate levels.

General Business

ELECTION OF OFFICERS

The following elections were made by the Council:

CHAIRMAN
The Revd Canon Colin Craston (England)

VICE-CHAIRMAN
The Revd Canon Simon E. Chiwanga (Tanzania)

MEMBERS OF STANDING COMMITTEE
Mrs Betty Govinden (Southern Africa)
The Most Revd Douglas Hambidge (Canada)
The Right Revd Alexander J. Malik (Pakistan)

REPORT OF
THE INTER-ANGLICAN FINANCE COMMITTEE

History and background

ACC-7 Resolution 34 of May 1987 called for the introduction of an Inter-Anglican Budget, provided the Lambeth Conference agreed. This Resolution was therefore brought before the Lambeth Conference 1988, which endorsed it, as Resolution 54 (*The truth shall make you free,* p 234). Following this, the matter was further discussed by the Primates' Meeting at Larnaca, Cyprus, in May 1989. The Primates also endorsed the concept, and established an Inter-Anglican Finance Committee to manage the budget on behalf of the Primates, the Lambeth Conference and the Anglican Consultative Council. The Right Revd L.E. Luscombe was invited to become its first Chairman.

The Committee met for the first time in March 1990. The Revd Canon Colin Craston was elected Vice-Chairman and the membership was as follows:

Elected by the Primates: The Right Revd L.E. Luscombe, the Most Revd George Browne

144

Elected by the ACC: The Revd Canon Colin Craston, the Venerable Yong Ping Chung, Mrs Pamela Chinnis, Mr David McIntyre
The Secretary General, the Revd Canon Samuel Van Culin, the Revd Michael Sams and the executive staff were in attendance.

Constitution

It quickly became apparent that, for this Committee to function effectively and legally, some simple constitutional arrangements were necessary. In consultation with Messrs Winkworth and Pemberton, the London solicitors of the Anglican Consultative Council, it was agreed that the simplest way to accomplish this would be to propose certain amendments to the Constitution and Byelaws of the Anglican Consultative Council. The basic reason for this was that neither the Lambeth Conference nor the Primates' Meeting have a constitution, and in fact are merely meetings. The ACC, however, has a Constitution, and the best way forward appeared to be to provide for the Inter-Anglican Finance Committee within it. Moreover, the office of the ACC had already become the central secretariat of the Anglican Communion, and the Primates at their meeting in Larnaca were anxious that this should be recognised.

Arising out of the introduction of the Inter-Anglican Budget and the constitutional amendments, and recognising the ACC's offices as the central secretariat of the Anglican Communion, a new letterheading for the ACC has been prepared.

Audited accounts for 1989

The audited accounts for the Anglican Consultative Council in respect of the year to 31 December 1989 were circulated to members for formal adoption by ACC-8. The significant figures in the accounts are as follows:

(a) The Council sustained a deficit of just over £3,000 for the year. This deficit was due to a combination of:

(i) A shortfall of contributions from member Churches which, at the date of the accounts, amounted to £48,318. Fortunately, since the date of the accounts some £17,000 has been recovered, but there still remains over £30,000, the prospect of recovering which is doubtful. We were helped during the year by receiving almost £30,000 of contributions unpaid in the previous year. Clearly, however, the payment of contributions is for some Churches a major difficulty, and because of that the Committee gave considerable thought to a revision of the schedule of contributions. This is discussed separately below.

(ii) An increase in expenditure for the year of over £8,000. The main element of the increase was in rent and service charges (over £8,000), following the move into new premises at Partnership House in Waterloo Road. There were increases in some employment costs, but these were largely offset by economies in other areas such as travel, hospitality and office expenses.

(b) The deficit for the year has been borne by the General Reserve, which now stands at some £28,000 below the level set by the Council under Resolution 49 of ACC-6. The Committee earnestly hopes that member Churches will make every effort to see that the budget contributions requested of them are paid in full, so as to restore the Council's General Reserve to the level set by the Resolution, i.e. one-third of the annual secretariat expenses.

(c) The Standing Committee of the ACC agreed to a request from the Primates' Meeting at Larnaca in 1989 to allocate just over £20,000 from the Inter-Anglican Theological and Doctrinal Commission Fund to meet the expenses of the third meeting of the Archbishop of Canterbury's Commission on Communion and Women in the Episcopate, and also the administrative costs of the Primates' Meeting. The rationale for this was that:

(i) both meetings covered substantial ground that otherwise would have formed the basis of major work for the IATDC;

(ii) mainly because of this, the appointment of a new IATDC has been deferred, thus releasing the funds.

Estimated outturn for 1990

For the information of members, and to act as a link between the accounts for 1989 discussed above and the budgets for the next triennium (1991-93) dealt with below, an estimate of the expected outturn for 1990 is appended, alongside the actual outturn for 1989 and the budgets for the next triennium. When the Committee met it appeared that there would be a deficit of something over £12,000, and they spent some time working together with the Secretary General and his staff to make further economies towards closing this gap. If member Churches met their contributions in full the gap would indeed be closed. Partly because of the threatened deficit, it was decided to leave the post of Associate Secretary for Mission and Social Issues unfilled for the time being, and major cuts were made in the Ecumenical department, in respect of both the Anglican Centre in Rome and inter-Church conversations.

However, one of the factors with which we have to contend is the increasing rate of inflation in the United Kingdom, as well as the weakness of sterling. Both these have the effect of increasing costs, and in particular put pressure on employment costs. On the other hand, high interest rates in the UK help to ensure an increased income from interest on deposits. In order to assist in the elimination of a deficit and the restoration of the Council's reserves, the Committee recommends continuing to sublet some of the office space at the central secretariat, while recognising that this creates difficulties for the secretariat staff.

Budgets for 1991-93

Draft budgets for the next triennium are tabulated below. These were drawn up after very careful consultation by the Committee together with the executive staff, and also after an extensive review of the implications of the Resolutions passed by ACC-6 and ACC-7, the Lambeth Conference of 1988 and the Primates' Meeting of 1989. Together we attempted to reflect on the major developments which have taken place on the inter-Anglican scene over the last decade, and sought to formulate budgets which respond to these developments and the various inter-Anglican meetings.

Considerable work has already been initiated in response to these various resolutions, in spite of very severe budgetary limitations. This has been made possible by generous help, both from Churches in seconding staff and from individuals who are prepared to work for the secretariat in a voluntary capacity. The Committee wishes to express warm thanks to these individuals and Churches.

The Revd Canon Robert Renouf was seconded by the Episcopal Church in the USA as Adviser for the Decade of Evangelism until the middle of 1991.

The Anglican Church of Canada has released the Revd Paul Gibson on a part-time basis as Liturgical Co-ordinator, to monitor and assist with the co-ordination of liturgical developments and information throughout the Communion. Though based in Canada he will be visiting the secretariat from time to time.

Through the generous funding of Trinity Church, Wall Street, New

York, in the USA, the Revd Fred Howard has been working as Director of the Inter-Anglican Information Network, following Resolution 53 of the Lambeth Conference (*The truth shall make you free,* p 234). This was referred to in the opening address of the Secretary General to ACC-7 in Singapore.

The Revd Canon Geoffrey Cates has been working in the office as a volunteer, helping to fill the gap created by the Revd Canon Martin Mbwana's long illness and subsequent death.

The Revd David Chaplin has also been working as a volunteer on constitutional issues.

The Committee is deeply grateful for these various secondments and volunteers, without which much of the work reflected in this Report would not have been done. Nevertheless such voluntary work creates additional demands on the office, in terms of space, secretarial resources and general office services. This has been taken into account in the budgets for the next triennium, but, in view of the financial situation, no provision has been made for the establishment of an Anglican Communion Liturgical Commission, as called for by Resolution 12 of ACC-7. The Revd Paul Gibson, in consultation with the voluntary Anglican Liturgical Consultation, will endeavour as far as possible to achieve the objectives of Resolution 12.

In accordance with Resolution 34 of ACC-7, the Inter-Anglican Budget now makes provision for the costs of the Primates' Meetings and the next Lambeth Conference. This initially appears to make the budget very much bigger; however, it must be borne in mind that these are not new items, but they have merely been consolidated into one main budget. Previously the member Churches of the Communion had been contributing to these costs under separate heads. Looked at in this light, the increase is not so great.

However, it must be stressed that the Inter-Anglican Budget does not provide for the cost of travel of bishops (or bishops' wives) to the Lambeth Conference. But we hope that, given the time before the next Lambeth Conference, each Diocese will be able to include in its annual budgets sufficient sums to meet these costs.

Every effort has been made to keep the costs of the central secretariat as low as possible, consistent with providing the standard of service which member Churches expect from it and with implementing the various resolutions passed by the three inter-Anglican bodies.

Revision of contribution schedule

Following Resolution 33 of ACC-7, one of the first tasks of the Committee was to review the way in which the total Inter-Anglican Budget was shared amongst the member Churches. A number of factors had to be taken into account. Over the past ten years or so, since the contributions schedule was last revised, a number of developments had taken place in the Anglican Communion and in the experience of individual member Churches. Some Churches, particularly in the so-called third world, are growing fast; new Provinces such as the Philippines are coming into being; the United Churches of the Indian sub-continent are coming into a closer relationship with the various Anglican bodies. On the other hand, some member Churches are going through periods of particular difficulty and it was clear that the amounts asked of them needed to be revised. After studying various statistics relating to membership and wealth in the Communion, it was quickly decided that a major revision of the schedule was neither practicable nor desirable.

The Committee sought therefore to make as few changes as possible while achieving the objective of relieving pressure on those member Churches where the amount requested was plainly too heavy a burden, and asking other Churches to make a small additional contribution (see table on p 156).

Following the adjustment of the schedule of contributions, however, a number of member Churches signalled their inability to meet these contributions even on the revised basis. As a result the Inter-Anglican Finance Committee recommended some amendments to the budgets in order to meet the anticipated shortfalls. These were agreed by ACC-8 (see Resolution 31 on p 167). The details are set out following the final summary financial statement on p 155.

INTER-ANGLICAN CORE BUDGET 1992
INCOME

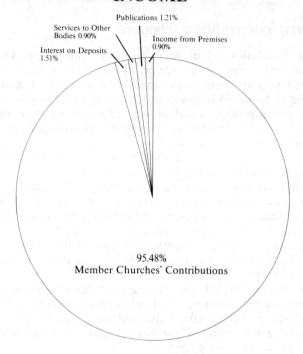

Publications 1.21%

Services to Other
Bodies 0.90%

Income from Premises
0.90%

Interest on Deposits
1.51%

95.48%
Member Churches' Contributions

EXPENDITURE

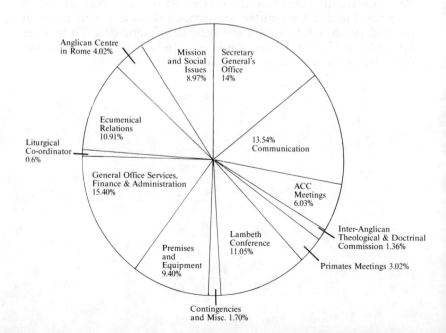

Anglican Centre
in Rome 4.02%

Mission
and Social
Issues
8.97%

Secretary
General's
Office
14%

Ecumenical
Relations
10.91%

13.54%
Communication

Liturgical
Co-ordinator
0.6%

General Office Services,
Finance & Administration
15.40%

ACC
Meetings
6.03%

Inter-Anglican
Theological & Doctrinal
Commission 1.36%

Premises
and
Equipment
9.40%

Lambeth
Conference
11.05%

Primates Meetings 3.02%

Contingencies
and Misc. 1.70%

FINANCIAL STATEMENT

INCOME

	ACC		INTER-ANGLICAN BUDGET			
	Actual outturn 1989 £	Budget (revised) 1990 £	Est. outturn 1990 £	Budget 1991 £	Budget 1992 £	Budget 1993 £
Interest on deposits	36,125	20,000	30,000	20,000	15,000	15,000
Received for services to other bodies	47,750	38,500	38,500	13,500	9,000	3,000
Publications sold	10,813	9,000	10,000	11,000	12,000	13,000
Grant for information technology equipment	13,125	12,500	12,500	—	—	—
Donations & miscellaneous	1,422	—	—	—	—	—
Contributions towards office relocation costs	9,000	9,000	9,000	9,000	5,000	—
Rent receivable	2,295	—	2,300	3,000	4,000	4,000
	£120,530	£89,000	£102,300	£56,500	£45,000	£35,000

FINANCIAL STATEMENT

EXPENDITURE

	ACC			INTER-ANGLICAN BUDGET		
	Actual outturn 1989	Budget (revised) 1990	Est. outturn 1990	Proposed Budget 1991	Proposed Budget 1992	Proposed Budget 1993
	£	£	£	£	£	£
Secretary General's office						
Employment costs	84,739	92,000	95,000	105,000	115,000	135,000
Recruitment costs	—	—	—	—	8,000	5,000
Hospitality	2,678	3,150	2,750	2,500	2,700	2,900
Travel	6,743	8,400	7,300	6,500	7,000	7,500
Housing	5,827	7,350	6,350	6,000	6,500	7,000
	99,987	110,900	111,400	120,000	139,200	157,400
Communication						
Employment costs	64,018	64,000	66,000	75,600	93,000	102,500
Hospitality	291	350	350	250	300	350
Travel	1,993	5,250	3,250	4,000	4,300	4,650
Publications	19,869	20,000	20,000	23,000	30,000	32,350
Books and journals	1,499	1,550	1,550	1,600	1,750	1,875
Translation grants	—	—	—	5,000	5,375	5,775
	87,670	91,150	91,150	109,450	134,725	147,500
Mission and Social Issues						
Employment costs	36,272	44,000	41,500	50,000	59,000	64,500
Recruitment costs	—	—	5,000	—	—	—
Hospitality	—	200	200	250	300	350
Travel	3,038	5,250	3,250	5,650	6,000	6,675
Provision for MISAG-2	10,000	10,000	15,000	7,500	8,000	10,000
Decade of Evangelism:						
Publications	—	—	3,500	3,500	4,000	6,000
Consultations	—	—	—	—	12,000	12,000
	49,310	59,450	68,450	66,900	89,300	99,525
Liturgical Co-ordinator support	—	—	—	1,000	6,000	6,500

EXPENDITURE (continued)

	ACC			INTER-ANGLICAN BUDGET		
	Actual outturn 1989 £	Budget (revised) 1990 £	Est. outturn 1990 £	Proposed Budget 1991 £	Proposed Budget 1992 £	Proposed Budget 1993 £
Ecumenical Relations						
Employment costs	48,790	49,500	53,000	58,300	64,000	70,500
Hospitality	279	150	250	250	300	350
Travel	5,016	3,750	3,750	4,000	4,300	4,650
Provision for inter-Church conversations	43,500	46,500	44,500	28,000	40,000	50,000
Anglican Centre in Rome	56,000	56,000	48,000	40,000	40,000	42,250
	153,585	155,900	149,500	130,550	148,600	167,750
Research	1,500	1,650	1,650	1,800	2,000	2,200
Administration and Finance						
Employment costs	75,787	78,000	86,000	93,000	102,250	112,500
Travel	1,721	3,000	3,000	3,000	3,500	3,725
Office expenses	28,317	40,000	38,000	36,000	38,750	41,600
	105,825	121,000	127,000	132,000	144,500	157,825
Audit and other professional fees	6,250	7,250	7,250	8,000	8,800	9,600
Office rent and maintenance	68,240	62,000	67,000	61,000	81,000	82,000
Depreciation:						
Office furniture	9,000	9,000	9,000	9,000	—	—
IT equipment	13,125	12,500	12,500	12,500	12,500	12,500
Seconded staff	3,857	—	—	—	—	—
Contribution to President's staff	750	750	750	825	900	1,000
Provision for contingencies *	—	8,450	—	15,500	14,000	11,500
Central Secretariat costs	£599,099	£640,000	£645,650	£668,525	£781,525	£855,300

* For unknown items, unexpected increases, losses on exchange or unpaid contributions etc.

153

SUMMARY FINANCIAL STATEMENT

	ACC		INTER-ANGLICAN BUDGET		
	Actual outturn 1989 £	Est. outturn 1990 £	Proposed Budget 1991 £	Proposed Budget 1992 £	Proposed Budget 1993 £
Total costs of Secretariat (p 153)	599,099	645,650	668,525	781,525	855,300
LESS Income (p 151)	120,530	102,300	56,500	45,000	35,000
	478,569	543,350	612,025	736,525	820,300
Provision for meetings (direct costs only)					
ACC (3-year cycle)	60,000	60,000	60,000	60,000	60,000
'Eames' Commission/Inter-Anglican Theological & Doctrinal Commission	11,000	12,000	13,000	13,500	14,000
Primates' Meetings	—	15,000	45,000	30,000	30,000
Lambeth Conference 1998	—	100,000	105,000	110,000	115,000
NET TOTAL	£549,569	£730,350	£835,025	£950,025	£1,039,300
Deficit	(3,163)	(12,350)			
Contributions received	£546,406	£718,000			

NOTE
By Resolution 31 (p 167 below), ACC-8 accepted the following reductions in the proposed budgeted expenditure for 1991 and 1992, as recommended by the Inter-Anglican Finance Committee in order to meet anticipated shortfalls in contributions from some member Churches in those years.

	1991 £	1992 £
Secretariat costs		
Communication		
Non-appointment of new staff	—	13,000
Mission and Social Issues		
Rescheduling appointment of MSI Associate Secretary *or* funding outside core budget: Employment costs	31,000	—
Ecumenical relations		
Rescheduling inter-Church conversations	—	15,000
Reduction in grant: Anglican Centre in Rome	—	4,000
	31,000	32,000
Provisions for meetings		
Anglican Consultative Council		
Deferring joint meeting of ACC-9 with Primates to January 1994	13,000	13,000
Primates	3,000	3,000
Inter-Anglican Theological & Doctrinal Commission		
Appointment of new commission deferred	13,000	13,500
Lambeth Conference: reduction in provision	20,000	24,000
	£80,000	£85,500

INTER-ANGLICAN BUDGET

PROPOSED REVISED PERCENTAGE CONTRIBUTIONS 1992

	%		%
Australia	10.50	Scotland	1.50
Brazil	0.50	Southern Africa	2.00
Burma (Myanmar)	0.10	Southern Cone of South America	0.25
Burundi, Rwanda, Zaire	0.20	(member Churches to decide individual	
Canada	11.00	allocations)	
Central Africa	1.25	Sudan	0.25
Ceylon	0.10	Tanzania	0.75
Council of Churches of East Asia	1.00	Uganda	1.00
(member Churches to decide individual		USA	27.25
allocations)		Wales	2.25
England (incl. Diocese in Europe)	28.15	West Africa	0.35
Indian Ocean	0.25	West Indies	1.50
Ireland	2.25	United Churches	
Japan	1.25	Bangladesh	0.06
Jerusalem & Middle East	0.50	Church of North India	0.10
Kenya	1.50	Church of Pakistan	0.10
Melanesia	0.10	Church of South India	0.15
New Zealand	3.00	Extra-provincial Dioceses	
Nigeria	1.50	Bermuda	0.10
Papua New Guinea	0.10	Lusitanian Church	0.05
Philippines	0.50	Spanish Reformed Episcopal Church	0.05
			101.46

Resolutions of ACC-8

Resolution 1: Christian spirituality
This Council urges every Diocese in our Communion to consider how through its structures it may encourage its members to see that a true Christian spirituality involves a concern for God's justice in the world, particularly in its own community.

Resolution 2: Staff resources for spirituality and justice issues
Among the priorities in its Inter-Anglican Budget this Council should provide staff resources for co-ordinating work on spirituality and justice issues within the Communion.

Resolution 3: Areas of concern and crisis
This Council calls the attention of its member Churches to the following areas of concern or crisis which have presented themselves to us with urgency during our time together, and urges, through study and the sharing of its results throughout the Communion, action where appropriate.
—SOUTH AFRICA, a nation which struggles to reach a negotiated solution to the rank injustice of apartheid, and to whose Church and people at this crucial time we offer our continued solidarity, support and encouragement;
—KENYA, where Church leaders are deeply concerned about curtailment of freedom of expression, massive rigging of elections and detention without trial;
—ISRAEL AND THE OCCUPIED TERRITORIES, where the Palestinian people struggle to maintain their dignity and integrity under inhuman conditions;
—CENTRAL AMERICA, whose agony is not yet over, and whose fragile peace is threatened both by economic ruin and deeply entrenched systemic injustices;
—PANAMA, where unnecessary military force was used by a superpower to deal with an internal conflict;
—nations whose INTERNATIONAL DEBT is paid with poverty, hunger and death, and whose people despair of the birthright of all God's children;
—SRI LANKA, which, like NORTHERN IRELAND, endures

157

chronic bloodletting, the end of which is not yet in sight;
—EASTERN EUROPE, in whose revolutions lie seeds of great hope which, ironically, carry also the threat of drawing away resources from the 'developing world', thereby widening the scandalous gap between the rich and the poor;
—SUDAN, where war, hunger and disease mount month by month, and whose Church calls out ever more urgently for the understanding and support of its partners-in-mission;
—INNOCENT VICTIMS of government wrath in several countries under authoritarian rule, some of whom have been summarily executed;
—the KOREAN NATION, tragically divided into two through no fault of its own, yearning for reunification and the harmony of its people;
—TRINIDAD AND TOBAGO, whose people have been suddenly confronted, in this time we have met here together, with a crisis yet to be worked through, and whose Church requests our prayers;
—MOZAMBIQUE, where people lose life daily as a direct consequence of war and hunger, and where the Churches have been praying and working, and requesting prayers and support, for peace and reconciliation.

Resolution 4: Liberia
This Council urges the Secretary General of the United Nations to use all his powers to bring to a speedy conclusion the fighting in Liberia, guaranteeing safe passage to refugees, and basic human rights to all the people of Liberia at this unsettled time.

Resolution 5: The South Pacific
This Council, noting that the people of the South Pacific, far removed from mass-media attention, face the economic and ecological ravages of drift-net fishing, the dangers in dumping nuclear wastes and poisonous gases, and continued testing of nuclear weapons by great powers, urges upon the Secretary General of the United Nations its concern for an immediate end to these practices.

Resolution 6: Prayers answered
This Council is thankful to God for many signs of encouragement since its last meeting in Singapore, noting that during these last three years the prayers of God's people have been answered in such events as the release of Nelson Mandela, the independence of Namibia and the fall of the Berlin Wall with all that it signified.

Resolution 7: Calendars of the Churches
This Council:
(a) receives the recommendations of the Lambeth Conference 1988 in its Resolution 60 (Recognition of Saints) to discuss the proposal by Africa Region, that the Anglican Communion should recognise men and women who have lived godly lives as saints, by including them in the calendars of the Churches for remembrance; and
(b) instructs the Co-ordinator for Liturgy, after consultation with the International Anglican Liturgical Consultation and research into earlier documentation and existing practice in some member Churches, to prepare guidelines for the recognition of men and women who have lived godly lives, by including them in the calendars of the Churches, and to submit these guidelines to the Standing Committee before disseminating them among the Churches as advice.

Resolution 8: Communion of the baptized but unconfirmed
This Council:
(a) notes that the Lambeth Conference 1988 in its Resolution 69 (Admission to Communion) has requested all Provinces to consider the theological and pastoral issues involved in the admission of those baptized but unconfirmed to Holy Communion, and to report their findings to the Secretariat;
(b) instructs the Co-ordinator for Liturgy to remind the member Churches of this request, and to arrange for the collation of their responses for submission to ACC-9.

Resolution 9: ACC Co-ordinator for Liturgy
This Council expresses its appreciation of the action of the Anglican Church of Canada in enabling the appointment to the Anglican Consultative Council staff of the Revd Paul Gibson as part-time Co-ordinator for Liturgy.

Resolution 10: Third International Anglican Liturgical Consultation
This Council:
(a) receives with appreciation the statement 'Down to earth worship' (Appendix I on p 172 below), commends it and the companion essays of *Liturgical inculturation in the Anglican Communion* to the member Churches for study, invites them to send responses and further examples of liturgical inculturation to the Co-ordinator for Liturgy, and expresses appreciation to the members of the International Anglican Liturgical Consultation for their thoughtful and helpful work on behalf of the Communion;

(b) welcomes the Guidelines (Appendix II, p 177) set out in the findings of the third International Anglican Liturgical Consultation, and believes that the Consultations have a continuing and important role in addressing liturgical issues affecting the Anglican Communion.

Resolution 11: Justice, Peace and the Integrity of Creation

This Council commends the affirmations and covenants of the Justice, Peace and the Integrity of Creation meeting at the World Convocation in Seoul, and asks all member Churches to identify and share these points where they relate to their own urgent local concerns; it instructs the Anglican Peace and Justice Network

(a) to monitor the Anglican Communion's response and adherence to the Seoul covenants;

(b) to share stories of specific ways in which these issues are being tackled in different areas, how these can be supported, what we can learn from them, and what their implications are for our own witness;

(c) to develop the common historical and theological analysis needed and thus move towards a common Christian 'confession' on the global crisis;

(d) to make recommendations for further action to the Churches through the Anglican Consultative Council.

Resolution 12: Adviser for the Decade of Evangelism

This Council urges, in the light of the termination of the secondment of the Adviser for the Decade of Evangelism, that practical steps be taken by the Standing Committee to provide some form of gathering and storing of information by the member Churches during the Decade and beyond.

Resolution 13: Translation of ACC documents

This Council should be aware of the need for documents issued by the Council to be available in translation, and should seek to facilitate this through the member Churches.

Resolution 14: Status of circulated documents

This Council requests the Standing Committee to consider for future meetings of the Council the need to clarify the status of documents circulated, both to member Churches and to Council members, and the purpose of the discussion of them by the Council.

Resolution 15: Anglican–Lutheran relations

This Council resolves that the name of the Anglican–Lutheran international dialogue be changed from 'The Anglican–Lutheran International Continuation Committee' (ALICC) to 'The Anglican–

Lutheran International Commission', in response to Resolution 4.3 of the Lambeth Conference 1988 (*The truth shall make you free,* p 204) and the action of the Executive Committee of the Lutheran World Federation.

Resolution 16: Anglican–Orthodox relations
This Council resolves that the name of the Anglican–Orthodox Dialogue be changed from 'The Anglican/Orthodox Joint Doctrinal Discussions' (A/OJDD) to 'The International Commission of Anglican–Orthodox Theological Dialogue' (ICAOTD), in response to the unanimous request of the members of the Dialogue.

Resolution 17: The Filioque clause
This Council resolves, in response to Lambeth Conference 1988 Resolution 6.5 (Anglican–Orthodox relations) which recalls Resolution 35.3 of the Lambeth Conference 1978, and in view of the generally positive response of the Churches in considering the removal of the Filioque clause from liturgical texts, and believing it possible to establish the historic text of the Niceno-Constantinopolitan Creed by removing the Filioque clause without betrayal of the Anglican theological heritage, to recommend to the member Churches of the Anglican Communion that in future liturgical revisions of the Niceno-Constantinopolitan Creed the Filioque clause be omitted.

Resolution 18: The Anglican Centre in Rome
This Council, having carefully considered the report of the Primates' Special Committee on the Anglican Centre in Rome and the Primates' Standing Committee's comments thereon, together with the proposed alterations to the Constitution of the Centre from its Council, and other submissions from the Centre, wishes to affirm the importance of the Centre in the life of the Communion and its desire to see its work continued and maintained in the most appropriate and cost-effective way, and now asks the Council of the Centre to amend its Constitution with immediate effect so as to replace the existing Council and Executive Committee with a new Governing Body consisting of:
(a) the Chairman, who shall be either the Anglican Co-chairman of the Anglican Roman Catholic International Commission or his nominee from among the Anglican membership of the Commission;
(b) a person appointed by the Anglican Consultative Council;
(c) a person appointed by the Archbishop of Canterbury;
(d) the Secretary, who shall be the Ecumenical Secretary of the Anglican Consultative Council.

The Governing Body shall co-opt as a member a person with financial expertise, unless one of the above qualifies.

All powers, duties and responsibilities of the present Council shall be assumed by the new Governing Body.

The foregoing amendments to the Constitution have the full endorsement of this Council, which by this Resolution completes the ratification required by the Constitution of the Anglican Centre.

The new Governing Body shall review the work, *modus operandi* and financial structure of the Centre and library, draft an appropriate Constitution to reflect these changes, and seek ratification from ACC-9.

This Council agrees, subject to the above amendments being adopted, to make budgetary provision for the next three years for allocation of a maximum of £40,000 for each of 1991 and 1992, and £42,250 for 1993, on the understanding that the Governing Body will be completely responsible for funding as soon as possible within the three-year period, and no later than the end of 1993.

This Council also resolves that Dr Diane Maybee shall be the person appointed by the Anglican Consultative Council if and when the new Governing Body comes into existence.

Resolution 19: The care of God's creation

This Council resolves:

(a) that the Archbishop of Canterbury be invited to sign on behalf of the Council the 'Letter to our children' appearing within the report of Section IV (pp 127-130) and that it be sent forthwith to the member Churches, with the request that it be used as a means of promoting understanding and the sharing of practical action with regard to care of the environment;

(b) that the Standing Committee be asked to liaise with (i) the Anglican Youth Network and (ii) Anglican representatives to the assembly of the World Council of Churches in Canberra, with a view to programmes being developed throughout the Communion on the care of God's creation.

Resolution 20: The Anglican Encounter

This Council commends the Anglican Encounter to be held in Brazil in 1992 and encourages member Churches to arrange for participation in this event.

(Explanatory Note: Anglican Encounter is planned by women and men from the six Provinces and national Churches of the Americas, in response to the call of the World Council of Churches for an ecumenical Decade of Churches in Solidarity with Women.)

Resolution 21: Identity and authority in the Anglican Communion

This Council, having received the document 'The Anglican Communion: Identity and authority' together with responses to it from four member Churches, resolves that:

(a) continued consideration of the document by member Churches be encouraged, together with consideration of responses;

(b) it should be referred for further responses generally and in particular:

    (i) for theological exploration to the Inter-Anglican Theological and Doctrinal Commission (in line with clause 1 of Lambeth Resolution 18) and to member Churches;

    (ii) to the International Anglican Liturgical Consultation, MISAG-2 and the Peace and Justice Network;

(c) member Churches be requested to act as a network (with the assistance of the Secretariat) in keeping other member Churches informed of their responses to the document;

(d) the responses be collated by the Secretariat in due time for the issues to be further considered at ACC-9.

This Council welcomes the proposal for a closer relationship between the Council and the Primates' Meeting, but considers the role of both bodies should remain consultative, and for this reason regards the document 'Provincial constitutions: autonomy and interdependence', circulated to the Council, as premature.

This Council recommends that the proposed Common Declaration should be referred to the Inter-Anglican Theological and Doctrinal Commission for study and report to ACC-9, and that member Churches should be asked to respond to this document so that replies can be discussed by ACC-9.

Resolution 22: Agenda for the Council's meetings
This Council resolves that a list and description of matters referred to the Council by a previous meeting, by a member Church, by the Primates' Meeting, by the Lambeth Conference, or by any other body, be prepared for each meeting of the Council, and that member Churches be consulted in the preparation of the agenda for meetings.

Resolution 23: Inter-Anglican Information Network (IAIN)
This Council welcomes with gratitude the provision of funds from Trinity Church, Wall Street, New York, that has enabled the setting up of the Inter-Anglican Information Network. It further records its thanks to the Director, the Revd Frederick Howard, for the progress made in establishing communication links within this project. It notes that the present provision will end in June 1992, and hopes that further funding outside the Inter-Anglican Budget will be found by the Director before that date for continuation of the development.

With Dr Runcie, the Right Revd Sir Paul Reeves, representative at the United Nations of the ACC and the Archbishop of Canterbury from early 1991.

Resolution 24: United Nations

This Council, reiterating the thanks to the Episcopal Church USA expressed at ACC-7 for financial and administrative help in setting up Non-Governmental Organisation (NGO) affiliation status with the United Nations Organisation, and grateful for further help from the Diocese of New York, Trinity Church (Wall Street, New York), and General Seminary (New York), confirms and welcomes the appointment of the Right Revd Sir Paul Reeves as the Anglican Consultative Council representative for the years 1991-1993, expecting this appointment to have benefits for all member Churches.

It recognises that if after this triennial period a further appointment is to be made, funding from outside the Inter-Anglican Budget will be required.

Resolution 25: The Philippine Episcopal Church
This Council welcomes the Philippine Episcopal Church, hitherto a member of the Eighth Province of ECUSA, as the latest member Church of the Anglican Communion, and thus of this Council.

Resolution 26: Co-opted member
This Council asks the Standing Committee, after due consultation and consideration, to appoint a co-opted member to succeed Bishop Abellon.

Resolution 27: The Archbishop of Canterbury's Commission on Communion and Women in the Episcopate
This Council welcomes the *Report of the Archbishop of Canterbury's Commission on Communion and Women in the Episcopate* (Parts One and Two; popularly known as the Eames Report), and commends it to all member Churches for their study. It urges member Churches whose policies in this regard differ to strive to maintain as high a degree of communion as possible.

Resolution 28: Adoption of accounts for 1989
This Council resolves that the Report and Financial Statements of the Anglican Consultative Council for the year ended 31 December 1989, as approved by the Standing Committee of the Council and signed on its behalf by the Chairman and Vice-Chairman, should be, and that they are hereby, adopted by this Council.

Resolution 29: Amendment of Constitution and Byelaws
This Council resolves that:
(a) two new sub-clauses be added to clause 2 of the Constitution to read as follows:
'(a) to facilitate the co-operative work of the member Churches of the Anglican Communion.'
'(l) to assist the Inter-Anglican Finance Committee (as hereinafter defined), the Primates' Meeting and the Lambeth Conference as and when required to do so.'
The other sub-clauses of this clause to be re-referenced accordingly.
(b) Byelaws be amended, pursuant to clause 2(o) of the Constitution, as follows:
(i) In Byelaw 3(a) after the words 'financial affairs' there be added: 'and the financial affairs of the Inter-Anglican Finance Committee'.
(ii) In Byelaw 3(b) after the word 'reports' there be added: 'such documents to include full financial reports on the Inter-Anglican

Finance Committee, the Primates' Meeting and where necessary the Lambeth Conference'.

(c) the existing Byelaw 4 be deleted and replaced by the following, to be numbered 5:

'The Inter-Anglican Finance Committee in collaboration with the Standing Committee shall, in consultation with member Churches, be responsible for the annual Inter-Anglican Budget, which will include the costs of the Inter-Anglican Finance Committee, the Primates' Meeting and the Lambeth Conference, and shall keep members of the Council and member Churches informed of each year's budget, and about the forecast for each of the succeeding three years. In the light of those draft budgets the Council, in consultation with the Primates, shall determine the level of expenditure and the income required to meet its purposes. The contributions to the Inter-Anglican Budget shall be apportioned among the member bodies as in clauses (b) to (e) inclusive of the schedule of membership.'

(d) a new Byelaw be inserted to read as follows and be numbered 4:

'Inter-Anglican Finance Committee

(a) The Council in conjunction with the Primates' Meeting shall appoint a finance committee of at least five members, to be called the "Inter-Anglican Finance Committee", which shall be responsible for co-ordinating the finances required by the Council, the Primates' Meeting and the Lambeth Conference.

(b) The membership shall consist of at least two members appointed by the Primates' Meeting, and at least three members appointed by the Council.

(c) Members appointed by the Council shall take their place on the Committee as from the end of the Council Meeting at which they are elected, and their membership shall continue so long as they remain members of the Council. Members appointed by the Primates' Meeting shall serve as long as the Primates shall determine.

(d) The Inter-Anglican Finance Committee shall appoint from its own membership its Chairperson and Vice-chairperson.'

The remaining Byelaws shall be renumbered appropriately.

Resolution 30: Amendment to Resolution 29 of ACC-4

This Council resolves that Resolution 29 of ACC-4 shall be rescinded and instead the following shall replace it:

'**Meetings of the Primates and the Lambeth Conference**

The Secretary General and his staff shall be available to serve, as the Archbishop of Canterbury shall require, as staff for meetings of the Primates and Lambeth Conference. The ACC shall not be responsible for the expenses of the Primates' Meeting or the Lambeth Conference. The Primates' Meetings and the Lambeth Conference shall be responsible for expenses incurred on their behalf by the Secretary General and his staff.'

Resolution 31: Approval of Financial Report

This Council resolves that the Inter-Anglican Finance Committee Report, including budgets for for 1991, 1992 and 1993 is accepted subject to the following amendments, as recommended by the Inter-Anglican Finance Committee, required in order to meet the anticipated shortfalls in contributions from some member Churches in 1991 and 1992:

	1991 £	1992 £
Secretariat costs		
Communication		
Non-appointment of new staff	—	13,000
Mission and Social Issues		
Rescheduling appointment of MSI		
Associate Secretary or Funding outside		
core budget: Employment costs	31,000	—
Ecumenical relations		
Rescheduling inter-Church conversations	—	15,000
Reduction in grant: Anglican Centre in		
Rome	—	4,000
	31,000	32,000
Provisions for meetings		
Anglican Consultative Council		
Deferring joint meeting of ACC-9 with		
Primates to January 1994	13,000	13,000
Primates	3,000	3,000
Inter-Anglican Theological and Doctrinal		
Commission		
Appointment of new commission deferred	13,000	13,500
Lambeth Conference		
Reduction in provision for next conference	20,000	24,000
	£80,000	£85,500

Resolutions

Resolution 32: Attendance of Chairman of the Inter-Anglican Finance Committee at meetings of the ACC Standing Committee
This Council resolves that the Chairman of the Inter-Anglican Finance Committee be invited to all meetings of the ACC Standing Committee.

Resolution 33: Voting procedures
This Council requests its Standing Committee to formulate for approval at ACC-9 Byelaws specifying procedures for elections and appointments required by the Constitution of the Council.

Resolution 34: Votes of thanks
(a) This Council gives thanks to God for the contribution of the following outgoing members who have served it faithfully. The Council assures them of its prayers.

Mr Maxwell F. Horton (Australia)
The Very Revd Walter Asbil (Canada)
Mr Gervase Chidawanyika (Central Africa)
Dr Margaret Hewitt (England)
Mrs Rhoda Lusaka (Kenya)
The Right Revd Samuel Ebo (Nigeria)
The Revd Canon John Kanyikwa (Sudan)
The Most Revd Edmond Browning (USA)
Mr David McIntyre (Wales)
The Right Revd Drexel Gomez (West Indies)
The Most Revd Richard Abellon (Philippines)

and in particular gives thanks for the work of the following members retiring from the Standing Committee:

The Most Revd Robert Eames (Ireland)
The Revd Canon Winston Ndungane (Southern Africa)

(b) This Council expresses its gratitude for the excellence of the Presentation Addresses made by:

The Right Revd Roger Herft
The Revd Professor Jaci Maraschin

(c) This Council gives thanks to the following Ecumenical Partners for their presence and participation and for their wise counsel and advice:

The Revd Dr Eugene Brand (Lutheran World Federation)
The Right Revd Sigisbert Kraft (Old Catholic Church)
The Revd Monsignor Kevin McDonald (Roman Catholic Church)

The Right Revd Philipose Mar Chrysostom (Mar Thoma Church)
The Revd Bernard Thorogood (World Council of Churches)
The Revd Dr Henry Wilson (World Alliance of Reformed Churches)

(d) This Council expresses its appreciation and gratitude to the Hosting Committee:
The Most Revd George Noakes (Chairman)
The Right Revd Roy Davies
Mr Glyn Ellis
The Venerable Barrie Evans
Mr John O. Evans
Mrs Dilys Fowler
Mrs Susan James
The Revd David Jones
Mr David McIntyre
Mrs Margaret McIntyre
Mr Wyn Mears
Mrs Jean Noakes
The Venerable Bryan Williams

(e) This Council expresses its appreciation and gratitude to the Editorial and Section Staff:
The Revd Dr Donald Anderson (ACC staff)
Mr Robin Brookes (Publisher)
Mr Roger Coleman (Editor)
Mrs Nicola Currie (ACC staff)
The Revd Paul Gibson (ACC staff)
The Revd Patrick Mauney (ECUSA)
The Revd Canon Stephen Platten (Lambeth Palace staff)
The Revd Canon Michael Rees (England)
The Revd Canon Robert Renouf (ACC staff)
Miss Charlotte Rivers (Australia)
Deaconess Margaret Rodgers (Australia)
Mr James Solheim (ECUSA)
Mr Douglas Tindal (Canada)
The Revd Canon Kenyon Wright (Scotland)

(f) This Council expresses its appreciation and gratitude to the following:
Communications team
Mr Michael Barwell (ECUSA)
The Revd Dr Robert Browne (ECUSA)

Mr Robert Byers (ACC staff)
The Revd Peter Davis (New Zealand)
The Revd Alun Evans (Wales)
Mrs Elizabeth Gibson-Harries (Ireland)
Miss Flavia Gonsalves (England)
The Revd David Jones (Wales)
Ms Estelle Marinus (Southern Africa)
The Revd Stanley Nyahwa (Central Africa)
Mr James Rosenthal (ACC staff)
Mrs Audra Surgeoner (Ireland)

Council staff team
Miss Lorraine Ashton
Ms Lisa Barnes
Mrs Helen Bates
Mrs Joan Christey
Mrs Elizabeth Coy
Miss Deirdre Hoban
The Revd Frederick Howard
Miss Marjorie Murphy
The Revd Canon Howard Root
The Revd Michael Sams
Mrs Rowena Small
Miss Janice Smith
The Revd Canon Roger Symon
The Revd Canon Samuel Van Culin
Ms Vanessa Wilde

Youth volunteers:
Miss Louise Cash
Mr Stephen Dunwoody
Miss Suzanne Wright

Chaplaincy team:
The Revd Margaret Harvey
Mrs Sue Oldroyd
The Right Revd Alwyn Rice Jones

Translators:
Miss Jean Dabinett
Mrs Susan James
Miss Euluned Morgan
Miss Mary Ridgewell
Miss Norma Westlake

(g) This Council expresses its appreciation and gratitude to the following:
   Mrs June Davis and all the staff at Dyffryn House and Gardens
   The Revd Henry Burlton, Chaplain, Heathrow Airport
   Mr Ajah Sodha and Key Travel
   The staff of Lloyds Bank

(h) This Council records its thanks to those member Churches which seconded Communications and Section Staff to facilitate this meeting of ACC-8.

Resolution 35: The Venerable Yong Ping Chung

This Council records its united and most affectionate gratitude to the Venerable Yong Ping Chung, its Chairman from 1984 to 1990, covering ACC-7 and ACC-8, and his service to the Council from ACC-4 in 1979. It has particularly valued his friendship and interest in all members, ensuring their concerns and needs are met from the earliest days of their membership, his patience, humour and fairness in chairing its meetings, his pastoral care for the ACC staff and his prayerful spirituality in leading all its affairs.

It has warmly welcomed his appointment as the Bishop of Sabah and prays for God's richest blessings on his ministry, in partnership with his wife Julia and his daughters Lois and Sarah, in the coming years.

Resolution 36: The Archbishop of Canterbury

This Council, representing the whole Anglican Communion, expresses to the Archbishop of Canterbury at this last meeting at which he will be President its united and deepest appreciation of his ministry to every member Church during his Presidency. His uniting and reconciling leadership, warm and gracious encouragement, cheerful and sensitive approach to fellow leaders and ordinary Church members in all parts of the world, rooted in devotion to his Lord, have enriched the Anglican Communion and many others beyond its membership.

The Council, drawn from many parts of the world, having experienced this ministry, has also admired the quiet dignity with which he has faced all situations, painful as well as pleasant, and gratefully acknowledges the moral authority he has always displayed.

The Council prays that he and Mrs Runcie will enjoy a long and satisfying retirement.

Appendixes

I. THE INCULTURATION STATEMENT

'DOWN TO EARTH WORSHIP': LITURGICAL INCULTURATION AND THE ANGLICAN COMMUNION

Findings of the Third International Anglican Liturgical Consultation York, England, 21-24 August 1989

Addressed to all those who worship God throughout the Anglican Communion, and for the special consideration of bishops, teachers of liturgy, and members of Liturgical Commissions. Circulated at the request of the Primates' Meeting of April 1989 to the ACC and Primates, for forwarding to the Churches of the Anglican Communion.

1   Introduction

From many parts of the world, we discovered afresh at York that liturgy to serve the contemporary church should be truly inculturated. Two of the Resolutions of the 1988 Lambeth Bishops encouraged us in this respect, and we begin from those Resolutions. We do not believe they have yet been sufficiently grasped in our Churches. But as we believe them to express the mind of God for Christian worship to-day, we underline and expand them here, and look and pray for their implementation.

2   Lambeth Conference Resolutions (each passed without dissent)

22   CHRIST AND CULTURE

This Conference (a) recognizes that culture is the context in which people find their identity; (b) affirms that. . . . the Gospel judges every culture . . . challenging some aspects of culture while endorsing others for the benefit of the Church and society; (c) urges the Church everywhere to work at expressing the unchanging Gospel of Christ in words, actions, names, customs, liturgies, which communicate relevantly in each contemporary society.

47   LITURGICAL FREEDOM

This Conference resolves that each Province should be free, subject to essential universal Anglican norms of worship, and to a valuing of traditional liturgical materials, to seek that expression of worship which is appropriate to its Christian people in their cultural context.

3 First principles

The incarnation is God's self-inculturation in the world, and in a particular cultural context. Jesus' ministry on earth includes both the acceptance of a particular culture, and also a confrontation of elements in that culture. When Jesus in turn commissions his disciples with 'As the Father has sent me, so I send you' they too are to pursue the mission which the Holy Spirit gives them by relating to their society incarnationally. They are to adapt themselves to different cultures ('as a Jew to the Jews, as a Greek to the Greeks') but also to confront the culture where it is contrary to the good news or to God's righteousness. Thus, just as language forms change from one place or time to another, so the whole cultural appropriateness of styles and expressions of worship should be ready to vary similarly.

4 Anglican starting points

Distinctive Anglicanism arose from the Church of England's break with Rome in the sixteenth century. The imposition then of a new and reformed liturgy contained *both* a principle of common prayer (which was appropriately expressed in the culture of its own times, not least in the use of Tudor English) *and* a general assertion of the freedom of Churches and Provinces in different places to develop their own distinctive forms (Art. XXXIV). We add that it is often the seeking of organic union or co-operation with other Christians which brings home to us our need to belong to our local culture for the sake of our mission.

5 Worldwide Anglicanism

The style of English Anglicanism, and even the actual wording of the 1662 BCP, have been frequently treated as being necessary features of being Anglican at all. But the weight of such a particular traditional Anglican culture (both of text and style) has also come to lie heavily upon the Churches in both urban England and rural Africa, in both South American cities and Asian villages. Even the modern revision of texts has often left styles unaltered, and has its own dangers of undue weight being attached to Western formulations. Our lack of inculturation has fostered both the cultural alienation of some Christians and an over-ready willingness of others to live in two different cultures, one of their religion and the other of their everyday life. Other Christians again have left our Churches because of this cultural insensitivity. Similarly non-Christians have found the foreignness of the church a great barrier to faith. The Lambeth 1988 Resolutions quoted above are designed to correct this situation.

6 Implementation

Inculturation must therefore affect the whole ethos of corporate worship, not only the texts but also, for example, the use of buildings, furnishings, art, music and ceremonial. From one aspect it means cultural de-colonization of worship, from another it requires recognition of the special needs of an ethnic or other minority, which may be culturally distinct from the prevailing ethos of the Province. True inculturation implies a willingness in worship to listen to culture, to incorporate what is good and to challenge what is alien to the truth of God. It has to make contact with the deep feelings of people. It can only be achieved through an open-ness to innovation and experimentation, an encouragement of local creativity, and a readiness to reflect critically at each stage of the process—a process which in principle is never ending. The liturgy, rightly constructed, forms the people of God, enabling and equipping them for their mission of evangelism and social justice in their culture and society.

For a Province or smaller unit to be creative and to adapt a received worship tradition with confidence and sureness of touch, it is greatly dependent upon both the liturgical scholarship and expertise of its leaders and teachers and the willingness of ordinary Christians to give and to receive in the inculturation process. We for our part long to see a better provision of well-equipped teachers and creators of liturgy through the Anglican Provinces, both in Colleges and in diocesan life, and a closer and more trusting relationship between bishops and synods on the one hand and well-equipped imaginative liturgists on the other.

7 Examples

We have discovered the need to illustrate these principles by examples. Those given here are necessarily few, for the sake of brevity, and are also inevitably arbitrary. Consider these questions:

(a) Language: is Tudor English anywhere appropriate to-day? Have countries developed local vernacular styles for liturgy? Are metaphors appropriate to the locality? Does the language exclude or demean any people on ethnic or gender or intellectual or other grounds? Are the kinds of book and the demands of reading them such that worshippers relate easily to them?

(b) Music: are English hymn-tunes universally appropriate? Do local musical styles provide a better cultural medium? Are local settings encouraged? Are the words of hymns, even if in translation, drawn from another culture? Is the organ all-pervasive, or are other instruments in use?

(c) Architecture: has Gothic with nave and chancel been over-valued worldwide? Can existing buildings be imaginatively adapted?

(d) Ceremonial: are choir-boys to wear surplices even on the Equator (and sit in those Gothic chancels)? Should robes be imported, or can they be locally designed with local materials? Are there ways in which people's existing practices can be incorporated? We heard of African dances in procession, of North American native peoples smoking the pipe of peace at the Peace, of workers in Sri Lanka bringing their union concerns and symbols into special eucharists, and the instances could be multiplied.

(e)   Sacramental elements: here there are special problems, needing more work. Should wafer bread be as dominant as it seems to be—even to the point of being imported? Should local staple food and drink supervene? How far can variations be allowed?

(f)   Rites of passage: we note the long-standing Christian Jando ceremony (male circumcision at the onset of puberty) in the diocese of Masasi, Tanzania, and its combination with confirmation and first communion. Is this a model to be copied or adapted elsewhere? Or are there other ways in which Christian initiation can be inculturated in different places? Equally, we sought examples of where local marriage customs have affected liturgy—but found few. Can such customs be more fully assimilated into marriage liturgies? The variety of culturally distinct styles of funerary customs is in process of rediscovery round the world, whether it be a Caribbean-style funeral in multi-ethnic parts of England or the Maori blessing of a house after a funeral in New Zealand.

(g)   Political and Social Context: at times Christians suffer or are oppressed, or are caught up in wars, or need to identify with the oppressed. This kind of stance, because it is their context, *becomes* their culture, and, if truly infusing their worship, in turn reinforces their public stance.

(h)   Agapes: Christians have gathered for meals from the start. The growing revival of agapes in our Communion we welcome, not only for the breaking down of walls between the 'sacred' and the 'secular', nor simply for their fellowship aspect, but also because both these factors enable people wherever they are to be themselves with their own customs, and to be free to bring those ways into the heart of church life.

We would not want to suggest that some purely 'tokenist' inclusion of a single local practice into an otherwise alien liturgy will suffice. Nor is it necessary for a whole liturgical event or series of events to be culturally monochrome: good liturgy grows and changes organically and always has rich marks of its stages of historical conditioning upon it, and in addition has often to serve truly multi-cultural congregations to-day.

In each Province and diocese Anglicans ought to examine their degree of attachment to ways of worship which are required neither by the gospel itself, nor by the local culture. We do not think that these criteria should be set aside by a loyalty to some supposed general 'Anglicanism', for *every* expression of the gospel is culturally affected, and what is viewed as general Anglicanism, if it can be identified, grew in a very specific Western culture.

8   Implications

Thus we believe that the Lambeth Resolutions (and the relevant parts of the Lambeth 'Mission and Ministry' section report (paras 180-186) call in question attempts to identify Anglicanism, whether locally or world-wide, through any common liturgical texts, ethos or style. We believe the 'essential

Anglican norms' of Lambeth Resolution 47 are largely those contained within the Lambeth Quadrilateral and described within Lambeth Resolution 18— i.e. the Bible, creeds, sacraments of the gospel, and episcopal ordination.* We believe the use of vernacular language to be foundational to inculturation, and within that value highly the 'traditional liturgical materials' to which Resolution 47 also refers. Our common liturgical heritage in items such as the Lord's Prayer promotes common prayer, sustains a dialogue with the scriptures, and conserves an element of the universal amid the particulars of inculturated worship.

The differing cultural styles of worship which are demanded by the above principles as between different Provinces and different parts of the world may also, on the same principles, be requisite *within* individual Provinces. Special encouragement should be given to minority groups, whether of ethnic or other composition, to develop their own culture in worship—and we applaud attempts made in various places (such as in the 1989 New Zealand Book) to bring minority cultures into the liturgical consciousness of majorities also.

We gladly acknowledge that true local cultural expression in worship has in some places gone far ahead of official provision. Sometimes this is to be found in the 'official' liturgy, sometimes outside of it; sometimes the desire to be untrammelled springs from the joy of charismatics or the fervour of the East African Revival, sometimes from more measured and careful introduction of truly local colour. In conformity with our main inculturation principles, we believe such ways should be welcomed, not wholly uncritically, but with a strong prejudice in their favour.

Our danger lies in inertia and in failure to recognize, understand, or value our own cultural contexts aright. Provinces should be ready both to treasure their received ways and also to reflect critically on them in the light of their own cultures. They should be wary lest sheer conservatism in liturgy, or an over-dependence upon uses from elsewhere, in fact become a vehicle of cultural alienation, making Anglican worship a specialist cult, rather than a people's liturgy. Let us hold fast to the essentials, and follow the cultural adaptability of the incarnation of our Lord Jesus in everything else.

9 Further stages

We also believe that some monitoring and reporting of the more general inculturation process could assist the whole Communion. Thus we request the Primates to report individually to the Steering Committee on positive progress made in inculturation in their Provinces. Particular examples will be greatly welcomed, and the Consultation itself has taken steps to promote circulation of such examples, together with a further discussion of the issues. In addition we hope that an overall report, to encourage the implementation of the Lambeth Resolutions, will be sent to each Province once a reasonably full set of replies has been received.

---

*   In Lambeth Resolution 18 (a lengthy consideration of issues of identity and authority in the Anglican Communion) paragraph 6 reads:

[This Conference] Requests the Archbishop of Canterbury, with all the Primates of the Anglican Communion, to appoint an Advisory Body on Prayer Books of the Anglican Communion. The Body should be entrusted with the task of offering encouragement, support and advice to Churches of the Communion in their work of liturgical revision as well as facilitating mutual consultation concerning, and review of, their Prayer Books as they are developed with a view to ensuring:

(a) the public reading of the Scriptures in a language understood by the people and instruction of the whole people of God in the scriptural faith by means of sermons and catechisms;

(b) the use of the two sacraments ordained by Christ, baptism with water in the threefold Name, and Holy Communion with bread and wine and explicit intention to obey our Lord's command;

(c) the use of forms of episcopal ordination to each of the three orders by prayer with the laying-on of hands;

(d) the public recitation and teaching of the Apostles' and Nicene Creeds; and

(e) the use of other liturgical expressions of unity in faith and life by which the whole people of God is nurtured and upheld, with continuing awareness of ecumenical liturgical developments.

Irrespective of the merits of an 'Advisory Body' (and in fact the Primates did not establish one), this Resolution represents an adherence by Lambeth 1988 to the principles of the 'Lambeth Quadrilateral'.

II. ANGLICAN LITURGICAL CONSULTATIONS GUIDELINES
Adopted at York, August 1989

Preamble

1. We welcome the recognition given to the International Anglican Liturgical Consultations (ALCs), particularly in Resolution 4 of the Standing Committee of ACC 1988 and in the presence of Bishop Colin James of Winchester as the Consultation's link with the Primates' Meeting and the ACC.

2. In view of the limited financial resources available for consultation on liturgical matters within the Anglican Communion and of the importance of establishing more effective means of communion within our Communion, we are grateful for the generosity of the Primate of the Church of Canada in making his Church's Liturgical Officer available to ACC, on a part-time basis, as a co-ordinator of communications about the liturgical concerns of the Provinces and regions of the Anglican Communion. ACC may wish to involve the ALC Steering Committee in the development of his job description.

3. We welcome the increasing awareness of the importance of consultation on liturgical matters within the Anglican Communion. We note with

appreciation ACC-7's recognition at Singapore of the second Anglican Liturgical Consultation and believe that regular Anglican Liturgical Consultations should be recognised as the significant place where liturgical issues affecting the whole Communion are addressed. Between these Consultations oversight of such issues will rest with the ALC Steering Committee.

Principles

1. The primary task of the Consultations is to foster mutuality, scholarship and understanding, to respond when particular issues arise and to assist clear communication, but not to impose any programme on the Anglican Communion.

2. Lambeth 1988 resolved that, 'each Province should be free, subject to essential universal Anglican norms of worship, and to a valuing of traditional liturgical materials, to seek that expression of worship which is appropriate to its Christian people in their cultural context' (Resolution 47).

It is part of the calling of Anglicanism to search for local expression in the worship of the historic Christian Church and to be committed to local ecumenism.

The Provinces and regional Churches of the Anglican Communion are self-governing. While Anglican Liturgical Consultations have no automatic authority within individual Provinces or their liturgical processes it is hoped that due weight will be given to their recommendations.

3. Links between ACC, the Primates' Meeting and the Anglican Liturgical Consultations are important and should be valued by all. This should promote healthy interaction between Provincial and regional leaders, those who have responsibility for liturgical processes within individual Churches, and liturgical expertise within the Communion.

4. The world of liturgical scholarship is increasingly ecumenical. It finds an international expression in the biennial meetings of Societas Liturgica. Holding ALCs in association with meetings of Societas Liturgica has advantages in terms of wide contacts and of financial savings. There should be no assumption that people must attend both events unless the theme of the Societas Liturgica meeting is of direct relevance to the ALC.

5. Consultations should be planned to promote:

(i) access to developments in liturgical scholarship and practice;

(ii) adequate representation of Provinces and regional Churches;

(iii) the contribution of those with expertise in particular areas;

(iv) mutual exchange, cross-fertilization and encouragement.

There is a need to balance continuity with open access and to avoid the formation of a closed group.

6. Funding for Consultations may remain limited for some time. A major claim on funds available from central sources should be enabling the attendance of those nominated by Provinces and regions unable to afford to fund participants for themselves. In addition, as recommended by the ACC Standing Committee, we hope that funds may be found from Churches attending previous Consultations to assist attendance from other Provinces and regional Churches.

We also welcome the suggestion of ACC-7 that support and funding should be offered to Provinces with few liturgically-trained specialists to help in pastoral and theological aspects of liturgy and in the training of liturgists.

Practice

1.   Biennial meetings in association with the meetings of Societas Liturgica should be the normal occasions for ALCs. This does not exclude the possibility of other meetings should occasions arise.

2.   Attendance should consist of:

(i)   those whom Provinces and regional Churches choose to nominate and send;

(ii) Anglican members of Societas Liturgica;

(iii) others whom the Steering Committee may invite.

3.   The business of ALCs should be directed by the Steering Committee and should include (but not be limited to):

(i)   items or themes determined by the Steering Committee;

(ii) matters referred by ACC or the Primates' Meeting;

(iii) matters referred by particular Provinces and regional Churches.

4.   The Steering Committee shall consist of:

(i)   three members elected at a Consultation;

(ii) one member of ACC appointed by the Standing Committee of ACC to be a link with ACC and the Primates' Meeting.

This Committee will elect from its own number a chairman and secretary within a period of three months from the conclusion of the Consultation.

5.   Much of the business of the Steering Committee will necessarily have to be done without the expense of face to face meetings. The ACC appointed co-ordinator may be invited to participate in ways that are deemed useful by the Steering Committee.

6.   The procedure for electing the three members of the Steering Committee shall be:

(i)   A nominating group of three people shall be elected at an ALC. Agreement to serve on this shall disqualify a person from being nominated to the Steering Committee.

(ii) The nominating group shall invite nominations for the Steering Committee and then present three names to the ALC for election. It shall take into account the diversity of regions and traditions of the Anglican Communion as well as practical considerations.

(iii) The ALC will have the right to make further nominations and will conduct a direct election.

(iv) At each election the person obtaining the most votes shall be elected for four years and the others for two years.

(v)   If a vacancy occurs the Steering Committee shall appoint a person to fill the office until the next ALC.

7.   The procedure of ALCs shall include the following:

(i)   The Steering Committee shall write after each Consultation to notify each Province or regional Church of the date of the next Consultation.

(ii) In preparation for Consultations the Steering Committee shall arrange for papers to be circulated in advance. It may also be helpful to arrange for the preparation of concise position papers on particular topics.
(iii) Consultations shall normally proceed by consensus.

III. OFFICERS AND MEMBERS OF THE ACC PARTICIPANTS AND STAFF AT ACC-8

OFFICERS

PRESIDENT	The Most Revd and Right Honourable Robert A. K. Runcie, Archbishop of Canterbury
CHAIRMAN	The Venerable Yong Ping Chung
VICE-CHAIRMAN	The Revd Canon Colin Craston
SECRETARY GENERAL	The Revd Canon Samuel Van Culin

MEMBERS

(The Sections to which members were assigned at ACC-8 are indicated in brackets after their names. The right-hand column shows the meeting of the ACC after which the member's term of appointment ends).

AUSTRALIA
The Most Revd Donald W. B. Robinson (II)	ACC-9
The Venerable Stuart M. Smith (III)	ACC-10
Mr. M. F. Horton (IV)	ACC-8

BANGLADESH
The Revd Birbal Haldar (III)	ACC-10

BRAZIL (IGREJA EPISCOPAL DO BRASIL)
The Right Revd Sumio Takatsu (IV)	ACC-10

BURUNDI, RWANDA AND ZAIRE
The Most Revd Samuel Sindamuka (I)	ACC-10
Mrs Josephine M. Rwaje (III) *[represented at ACC-8 by the Revd O. Rwaje]*	ACC-10

CANADA
The Most Revd Douglas Hambidge (I; Chairman, Identity & Authority group)	ACC-9
The Very Revd Walter G. Asbil (II, Chairman)	ACC-8
Dr Diane N. Maybee (IV)	ACC-10

CENTRAL AFRICA
The Very Revd R. A. B. Ewbank (IV)	ACC-8
Mr Gervase W. Chidawanyika (III)	ACC-8

CEYLON (SRI LANKA)
The Right Revd Andrew Kumarage (I)	ACC-9

EAST ASIA
  The Right Revd Tan Sri John Savarimuthu (I)   ACC-8
  Miss Angela Pang Che-Soon (II)   ACC-9

ENGLAND
  The Right Revd Colin W. James (II)   ACC-9
  The Revd Canon B. M. M. O'Connor (IV)   ACC-10
  Dr Margaret Hewitt (III)   ACC-8

INDIAN OCEAN
  The Revd Roger Chung Po Chuen (III)   ACC-10

IRELAND
  The Most Revd Robert Eames (III)   ACC-8
  The Venerable M.H.G. Mayes (IV)   ACC-10

JAPAN (NIPPON SEI KO KAI)
  The Right Revd Joseph J. Iida (IV)   ACC-9

JERUSALEM AND THE MIDDLE EAST
  The Right Revd John Brown (IV)   ACC-10

KENYA
  The Right Revd Dr David Gitari (IV)   ACC-9
  Mrs Rhoda Lusaka (I)   ACC-8

MELANESIA
  The Most Revd Amos Waiaru (II)   ACC-10

MYANMAR (BURMA)
  The Right Revd Samuel San Si Htay (I)   ACC-10

NEW ZEALAND
  The Revd John Paterson (II)   ACC-10
  Mr Edgar Bradley (IV, Chairman)   ACC-9

NIGERIA
  The Right Revd S.C.N. Ebo (IV)   ACC-8
  The Very Revd V.O. Muoghereh (III)   ACC-10
  The Honourable Mr Justice Christian A. Abimbola (I)   ACC-9

NORTH INDIA
  The Most Revd John E. Ghose (II)   ACC-10
  The Revd Noel S. Sen (I)   ACC-10

PAKISTAN
  The Right Revd Alexander Malik (IV)   ACC-10
  Mr Theodore Phailbus (III)   ACC-10

PAPUA NEW GUINEA
  The Revd Tevita Talanoa (III)   ACC-10

SCOTLAND
  The Very Revd Ian Watt (I)   ACC-9

SOUTHERN AFRICA
The Right Revd Dinis Sengulane (IV)   ACC-10
The Revd Canon Winston Ndungane (I, Chairman)   ACC-8
Mrs Betty Govinden (III)   ACC-9

SOUTHERN CONE OF SOUTH AMERICA (IGLESIA ANGLICANA DEL CONO SUR DE AMERICA)
The Revd Julio Bustos (II)   ACC-9

SOUTH INDIA
The Right Revd Dr D. Pothirajulu (III)   ACC-10
The Revd B.P. Sugandhar (IV)   ACC-10
Professor Samuel Kadakaseril (II) *[represented at ACC-8 by Professor G. Koshy]*   ACC-10

SUDAN
The Right Revd Daniel Zindo (III)   ACC-9
The Revd Canon John L. Kanyikwa (I)   ACC-8

TANZANIA
The Right Revd Charles Mwaigoga (IV)   ACC-10
The Revd Canon Simon Chiwanga (II)   ACC-10

UGANDA
The Right Revd G. Oboma *[not present at ACC-8]*   ACC-9
The Revd Canon Lusania N. Kasamba (I)   ACC-10
Mr Philmon Ameru *[not present at ACC-8]*   ACC-10

USA
The Most Revd Edmond Browning (II)   ACC-8
The Revd Austin R. Cooper (I)   ACC-10
Mrs Pamela Chinnis (III, Chairperson)   ACC-9

WALES
The Most Revd George Noakes (III)   ACC-9
Mr J.W.D. McIntyre (IV)   ACC-8

WEST AFRICA
The Most Revd George D. Browne *[unable to be present at ACC-8]* ACC-9

WEST INDIES
The Right Revd Drexel W. Gomez (I)   ACC-8
The Venerable Alvin E. Stone (II) *[represented at ACC-8 by Mr Ivan Jessamy]*   ACC-10

CO-OPTED MEMBERS
The Most Revd Richard Abellon (II)   ACC-8
Mrs Ruth Yangsoon Choi (I)   ACC-9
Mrs Faga T. Matalavea (II)   ACC-9
Mr César Guzmán (III)   ACC-9
Miss Lorna Helen (I)   ACC-9
The Right Revd James H. Ottley (II)   ACC-9

PARTICIPANTS FROM CHURCHES IN FULL COMMUNION
MAR THOMA SYRIAN CHURCH OF MALABAR
The Right Revd Philipose Mar Chrysostom
OLD CATHOLIC CHURCH
The Right Revd Dr Sigisbert Kraft

PARTICIPANTS FROM OTHER CHURCHES
LUTHERAN CHURCH
The Revd Dr Eugene Brand
ROMAN CATHOLIC CHURCH
The Revd Monsignor Kevin McDonald
WORLD ALLIANCE OF REFORMED CHURCHES
The Revd Dr Henry Wilson
WORLD COUNCIL OF CHURCHES
The Revd Bernard Thorogood

CONSULTANTS AND SPEAKERS
The Right Revd Roger A. Herft (New Zealand)
The Revd Professor Jaci Maraschin (Igreja Episcopal do Brasil)

STAFF
EDITORIAL AND SECTION STAFF
The Revd Dr Donald Anderson, Mr Robin Brookes, Mr Roger Coleman, Mrs Nicola Currie, The Revd Paul Gibson, The Revd Patrick Mauney, The Revd Canon Stephen Platten, The Revd Canon Michael Rees, The Revd Canon Robert Renouf, Miss Charlotte Rivers, Deaconess Margaret Rodgers, Mr James Solheim, Mr Douglas Tindal, The Revd Canon Kenyon Wright.

COMMUNICATIONS TEAM
Mr Michael Barwell, The Revd Dr Robert Browne, Mr Robert Byers, The Revd Peter Davis, The Revd Alun Evans, Mrs Elizabeth Gibson-Harries, Miss Flavia Gonsalves, The Revd David Jones, Ms Estelle Marinus, The Revd Stanley Nyahwa, Mr James Rosenthal, Mrs Audra Surgeoner.

COUNCIL STAFF TEAM
Miss Lorraine Ashton, Ms Lisa Barnes, Mrs Helen Bates, Mrs Joan Christey, Mrs Elizabeth Coy, Miss Deirdre Hoban, The Revd Frederick Howard, Miss Marjorie Murphy, The Revd Canon Howard Root, The Revd Michael Sams, Mrs Rowena Small, Miss Janice Smith, The Revd Canon Roger Symon, The Revd Canon Samuel Van Culin, Ms Vanessa Wilde.

YOUTH VOLUNTEERS
Miss Louise Cash, Mr Stephen Dunwoody, Miss Suzanne Wright.

CHAPLAINCY TEAM

The Revd Margaret Harvey, Mrs Sue Oldroyd, The Right Revd Alwyn Rice Jones.

TRANSLATORS

Miss Jean Dabinett, Mrs Susan James, Miss Euluned Morgan, Miss Mary Ridgewell, Miss Norma Westlake.

STANDING COMMITTEE

(The President is a member of the Standing Committee ex officio)

OTHER MEMBERS FOR ACC-8

The Venerable Yong Ping Chung (Chairman), The Revd Canon Colin Craston (Vice-chairman), Mr Edgar Bradley (New Zealand), The Most Revd George D. Browne (West Africa), Mrs Pamela Chinnis (USA), The Most Revd Robert Eames (Ireland), The Right Revd Joseph J. Iida (Japan), The Revd Canon Winston Ndungane (Southern Africa).

OTHER MEMBERS FOR ACC-9

The Revd Canon Colin Craston (Chairman), The Revd Canon Simon Chiwanga (Vice-chairman), Mr Edgar Bradley (New Zealand), The Most Revd George D. Browne (West Africa), Mrs Pamela Chinnis (USA), Mrs Betty Govinden (Southern Africa), The Right Revd Joseph J. Iida (Japan), The Most Revd Douglas Hambidge (Canada), The Right Revd Alexander Malik (Pakistan).

INTER-ANGLICAN FINANCE COMMITTEE

The Right Revd Edward Luscombe (Chairman), The Most Revd George D. Browne, Mrs Pamela Chinnis, The Revd Canon Colin Craston, Mr J.W.D. McIntyre.

IV. PREVIOUS MEETINGS OF THE COUNCIL

ACC-1	Limuru, Kenya, 23 February to 5 March 1971
	Report *The Time is Now* (out of print)
ACC-2	Dublin, Ireland, 17 to 27 July 1973
	Report *Partners in Mission*
ACC-3	Trinidad, 23 March to 2 April 1976
	Report of Third Meeting
ACC-4	London, Ontario, Canada, 8 to 18 May 1979
	Report of the Fourth Meeting 1979
ACC-5	Newcastle, England, 8 to 18 September 1981
	Report of Fifth Meeting
ACC-6	Badagry, Nigeria, 17 to 27 July 1984
	Report *Bonds of Affection* (out of print)
ACC-7	Singapore, 25 April to 9 May 1987
	Report *Many Gifts One Spirit*

Reports of ACC-2, ACC-3, ACC-4 and ACC-5 are available from the Anglican Consultative Council, Partnership House, 157 Waterloo Road, London SE1 8UT. *Many Gifts One Spirit* is obtainable through booksellers.

INDEX

Abellon, Most Revd R. 6, 165
ACC, role of 7, 31f, 56, 142, 163
ACC-4 36
ACC-6 37, 119
ACC-7 37, 148f, 171
ACC Constitution and Byelaws 145, 165
ACC membership v, 180ff
Advertising 69
AIDS 9, 20, 47, 80
Anglican Centre in Rome 14, 138f, 147, 161f
Anglican Communion 1, 4, 7, 12, 25ff, 36ff, 41, 54, 140ff
Anglican Encounter (Brazil, 1992) 131, 162
Anglican Liturgical Consultations 12ff, 46, 106f, 148, 159, 172ff
ARCIC 137, 161
Asbil, Very Revd W. 6, 47
Augustine of Canterbury, St 24f
Australia, Church of 9, 18
Authority (Anglican) 2, 11, 25f, 30, 32ff, 49, 140ff, 162f
Autonomy, provincial 4, 25, 32, 140

Bangladesh, Church of 1, 27f, 35, 113
Base communities 51, 115
Bible 29f, 44, 57, 73, 92, 95
Bible study 2f, 82, 91
Bradley, E. 45
Brazil, Episcopal Church of 7, 51, 53, 63
Browne, Most Revd G. 1, 5f, 19, 27, 47
Browne, Revd Dr R. 44, 126
Browning, Most Revd E. 5, 18, 53
Budgets, see Finance
Burma, see Myanmar
Bush, President G. 4, 35

Canada, Anglican Church of 46, 47, 147
Canterbury, role of Archbishop 7, 15, 25f, 29, 55, 142
Capitalism 60
Cardiff City Council 4
Carey, Rt Revd G. 15
Chaplaincy team 2f, 170
China, Church in 28
Chinnis, Mrs P. 43
Chiwanga, Revd Canon S. 16, 144
Civil rights movement (USA) 93
Coggan, Rt Revd Lord 19, 36, 44
Colonialism 55, 94
Common Declaration 143, 163
Communication 8, 21f, 43, 60, 112ff
Communication technology 4, 44
Communion 7, 20, 25f, 49, 54, 59ff, 141
Co-ordinator for Liturgy 107f, 159
Craston, Revd Canon C. 16, 38, 144
Creation, integrity of 20, 101ff, 127ff, 162
Creeds 57f, 161
Cursillo movement 115

Debt, international 103, 157
Decade of Evangelism 4, 8, 9, 12, 14, 40, 42f, 46, 51, 75, 86, 112ff, 133, 160
Denominationalism 54, 133

Diversity of Anglicanism 4, 23ff, 28ff
Dyffryn House and gardens 1, 6f

Eames, Most Revd R. 8, 16
'Eames Report' 14, 146, 165
Ebo, Rt Revd S. 18
Ecumenical Advisory Group 45, 137
Ecumenical Councils 33
Ecumenical relations 12ff, 16, 30, 45, 63, 131ff, 160f, 168f
Education and training 99, 108, 113, 123, 131, 133
Election of officers 16, 168
Environmental problems 12ff, 19f, 80, 127ff, 158
Episcopacy 32, 55f
Ethiopian Orthodox Church 28
Evangelism 11, 14, 40, 43, 71ff, 87, 112ff; see also Decade of Evangelism
Filioque clause 12, 161
Finance 16, 30, 39, 44, 139, 144ff, 163, 165ff, 178
Fishermen parable 75
Fundamentalism 13, 71, 138

General Theological Seminary 45
Gibson, Revd P. 46, 107, 147f, 159
Gitari, Rt Revd D. 6, 18
Government 97, 131
Govinden, Mrs B. 16, 18, 144
Grace 59, 68
Green movement 28, 71

Hambidge, Most Revd D. 2, 16, 144
Herft, Rt Revd R. 7f, 43, 64ff, 168
Howard, Revd F. 44, 148, 163
Human rights 11, 98f, 103
Humility 36, 96

Identity and authority (Anglican Communion) 2, 25, 49, 140ff, 162f
Inculturation of liturgy 11, 106, 159, 172
Inter-Anglican Finance Committee 16, 144ff, 165ff, 184
Inter-Anglican Information Network 5, 43f, 148, 163
Inter-Anglican Publishing Network 4, 43
Inter-Anglican Theological and Doctrinal Commission 141f, 146, 163
Inter-faith relations 13, 66, 77, 84, 89f, 124, 131, 137f
International Conference of Young Anglicans 46f
Ireland, Church of 8, 47
Isaiah Agenda 76f
Islam 18, 27, 137f

James, Rt Revd C. 46
Judaism 137
Justice 34, 47, 53, 80, 86ff, 102ff, 157
Justice, Peace and the Integrity of Creation, Convocation 11, 13, 102ff, 160

Kauluma, Rt Revd J. 26
Kenya 6, 27, 157
Koinonia 30f, 59; see also Communion
Korea 11, 13, 102ff, 158, 160
Kraft, Rt Revd S. 18

185

Index